Bottom Bunk –
Top Two Drawers

Bottom Bunk –
Top Two Drawers

Gerald Stevens

An account of the first voyage
by an apprentice aboard a
tramp ship in the early fifties.

The Pentland Press Limited
Edinburgh • Cambridge • Durham • USA

First published in 1998 by
The Pentland Press Ltd.
1 Hutton Close
South Church
Bishop Auckland
Durham

British Library Cataloguing in Publication Data.
A Catalogue record for this book is available
from the British Library.

ISBN 1 85821 564 1

Typeset by CBS, Felixstowe, Suffolk
Printed and bound in Great Britain by Bookcraft (Bath) Ltd.

To Stratton Long, of Blakeney

ACKNOWLEDGEMENTS

I would thank:

Judith Whitcher, the only person I've ever met who can read my longhand and type.

Henry Brown.

Ruth Clague, Craig McMath and the Receptionists at the Blakeney Hotel.

Matthew King, for pointing out that at least thirty pages of the original manuscript were bosh.
His cat 'Muffin' for guarding the spare manuscript.

John and Julie Loakes.

FOREWORD

I first met the author in 1980, but he is a quiet, reserved type and it was some years before we had any meaningful conversation. I discovered then that he possessed a sharp wit and a wicked sense of humour, but he does not suffer fools gladly.

We have now become firm friends and I enjoy his fund of stories as he recalls events in his life at sea.

As an author myself I am always interested in the writings of others and when he told me that he had composed a preliminary draft of his experiences I urged him to put it into book form. I think that I had the honour of being the first person to read the final manuscript and I found it both amusing and entertaining.

He informed me that it was still lacking the final chapter and I urged him to complete it. In fact I nagged him over a considerable period – so here it is. The record of the life of a young cadet in the Merchant Navy during the immediate post war years. I found it fascinating and encouraged him to find a publisher. So if you do not enjoy this book, blame me, not the author. I talked him into it.

Henry Brown F.R.I.C.S.
Chartered Surveyor
Sleaford, Lincolnshire

AUTHOR'S NOTE

It has been attempted to write this book with only the knowledge the author had at the time; so there is as little hindsight as possible, and it should be read as coming from a seventeen-year-old.

With hindsight, had I been Master of the ship at the time I would have thrown Gerald Stevens overboard after about five weeks and to hell with the paperwork!

THE AUTHOR

Gerald Stevens was born and bred in Norfolk. His first brush with salt water was when he was allowed to steer a sailing dinghy at the age of six. He was then in and out of every vessel (the word 'vessel' includes any description of craft used, or capable of being used, as a means of transportation on water; Article 1) he could.

At seventeen he joined the Merchant Service, ending up with a Master's Certificate. He wrote this book firstly because he had never read a book that gave a proper description of a first trip, and secondly to describe something that has gone.

He started by just missing coal-burning ships and ended by serving on Bridge Control ships with no one down below.

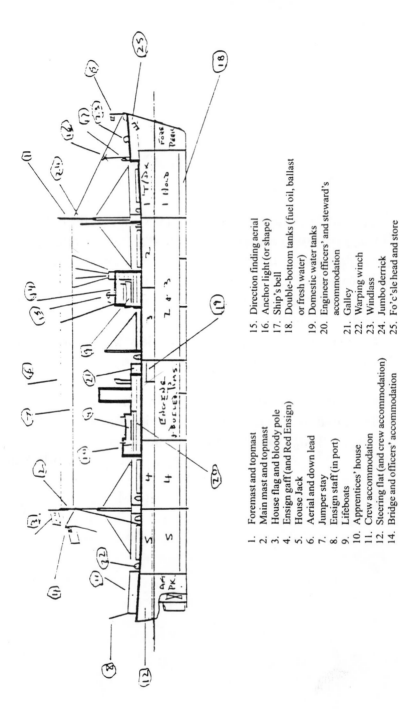

1. Foremast and topmast
2. Main mast and topmast
3. House flag and bloody pole
4. Ensign gaff (and Red Ensign)
5. House Jack
6. Aerial and down lead
7. Jumper stay
8. Ensign staff (in port)
9. Lifeboats
10. Apprentices' house
11. Crew accommodation
12. Steering flat (and crew accommodation)
14. Bridge and officers' accommodation

15. Direction finding aerial
16. Anchor light (or shape)
17. Ship's bell
18. Double-bottom tanks (fuel oil, ballast or fresh water)
19. Domestic water tanks
20. Engineer officers' and steward's accommodation
21. Galley
22. Warping winch
23. Windlass
24. Jumbo derrick
25. Fo'c'sle head and store

So there I was outside a Tyneside station, all uniform, brass buttons and cap badge. Ship too near for a taxi to accept the fare, and too far for a small deck cadet who had somehow ended up with three bits of heavy luggage. I started to leapfrog my gear towards the ship when I was overtaken by three large dockyard workers who, seeing my predicament, wrested my baggage from me and took it aboard ship. For three grown men to be that thoughtful towards a semi-lost youngster was a thing that impressed me deeply. Many seamen are prejudiced against Geordies. By their kindness, those men allowed me to meet future Geordies with a bias: pro.

Anyway, in spite of what everybody else thinks about Geordies, I was now aboard a British merchant ship as an Indentured Apprentice. Four years of it. Indentures were still taken very seriously by both parties at this time, not long after World War Two. The two curbs on apprentices seemed to be 'Shore leave stopped' or the Master saying 'I'll cancel your indentures.' The threat of cancelled indentures receded as one had so much stoppage of shore leave piled up that, unless one was allowed to serve one's time out, the leave stoppage would never have been worked off. I think I probably had several days stoppage to go when I was promoted Third Officer three years later. It always started with something innocent and then gently snowballed with leave stopped for going ashore while leave was stopped. I stress that discipline was very much in evidence, although Nelson was not the only officer who ever turned a blind eye, and we did get

1

ashore sometimes.

In any case, there was the indenture-signing ceremony at the Company Office, and the part read out was 'shall not enter ale houses or houses of ill repute except about the Master's business'. So, what the hell.

I had been warned that the first step was to report to the Chief Officer, usually called the Mate. He was a disappointed man. Mates love to look first-trip brassbound apprentices disdainfully up and down and then give the standard first order to what may turn out to be a brilliant career. 'Take that bloody lot off and get into working gear.' Unfortunately for him it was High Tea time minus five, so I was handed my cabin keys and told to go and eat.

The cabin was palatial compared with many cadets' cabins I was to see. Dayroom – long settee with drawers underneath, fixed table, two hard-backed padded chairs, two bookshelves, two deep cupboards for heavy weather gear, corticene deck and small bright piece of carpet. Through an adjoining door was a sleeping cabin – two wardrobes and two fore-and-aft bunks. When she rolled, all the drawers fell out. I have asked in my time all manner of superintendents, ship-builders and ship repairers why almost all bunks are fore-and-aft when athwartships are better to sleep in during heavy weather. In any case with an athwartships bunk when the drawers fall out it is time to call it a day. I once, for laughs years later, asked a naval architect about this fore-and-aft syndrome; he put on a serious smile and confided: 'A ship we have just designed has them throughout.'

My fellow apprentice arrived, another first-tripper whom I had met only briefly and in front of other people; within a couple of minutes I thankfully realised that he had the most glorious sense of humour.

A High Tea, called Tea, in the saloon was served to us at the bottom of the second table. Definitely below the salt. Until that time I had wondered about this expression. Nautically it was quite simple: if the pair of us did not behave impeccably at table throughout the trip, the bastards would not pass it down.

Tea over, it was back to the boat deck-house and unpacking, half wondering what was going to happen next. The Third Mate happened.

He was newly promoted and uncertificated: always known as 'uncertified', of course. Then we were introduced to a practice called 'flags and lights'. Lights had to go off as quickly in succession as we could get round the switches, at dawn. Flags should go up all at once at eight o'clock. We pointed out that there was a Jack forward, a House flag at the main, and a Red Ensign aft; when in a port abroad we would have that country's flag to fly at the foremast starboard yard-arm as well, and there were only two of us. The Third Mate relented, we started aft and worked forrard as fast as possible.

But now came the night. At sunset, starting from forrard, all flags down and all lights on. What a merry scamper. Naval architects love putting light switches into the darkest corners and at the end of long alleyways. With practice we took pride in being very fast.

The Third Mate's briefing continued. Wheel-house, chartroom and bridge care were to be our chief occupations. Leaving harbour one of us forrard and one aft. Dirty jobs would be ours, which we expected. The plot thickened and hatch bilges were mentioned. Our bilges bore a covering of sticky bitumastic. Few people working in a hatch bothered to come out to relieve themselves; the bilges were too handy. After two years, my mate and I reckoned to be able to tell the nationality of a piece of shit anywhere from Shanghai to Shangri-la, the long way round. We never did come across any Eskimos, but if tramp ships had flown over the pole, I am quite sure we would have done.

The Third Officer also explained the reason for double everything in our accommodation; obvious, no shared space, no arguments. The single washbasin was explained to the curious; just before the ship was built, the Officers' Association had insisted that wash basins be provided in each officer's cabin. They were. No taps, no master pipe, use the nearest bathroom – you would have to go there for water anyway.

The Third Officer rose to leave, obviously somebody whose dignity must never be infringed by us, but we knew we had at least one friend on board.

Next morning was not a happy time. The Mate had sent the newly promoted Third Mate to get the draught, much to several people's amazement. We were in dry dock! Obvious, one would think, but even knowing the scheme, I was caught later when I was new. The Third Mate was a bit purple for the rest of the day, and not throwing much information away, except of course to kick up hell when flags and lights were two minutes late.

I was always warned that cadets got the muck, and I thought I was ready for anything when the first job came up. It was a 'go with the Bo'sun' morning. The Bo'sun pointed at four tangled three-inch thick guy ropes and said, 'Clear those.'

Tangled they were, all in amongst a pile of muck which had the smell and consistency of twelve-hour-old cat spew. We got covered in it.

The next two or three days were a whirl of keen helpfulness on our part, but we just didn't know what was going on. Except that we still reeked of cat spew.

The morning came for signing on and a load of strangers appeared in front of the Board of Trade Shipping Master and the Old Man. Big, important ceremony. My part of it was to be presented to the Shipping Master, who then asked the Old Man for my indentures. Apprentices did not sign on; it appeared that everybody only wanted to check they had got the right indentures for the right cadet.

Leaving the dry dock, where I was sent aft to help, was a bit bewildering as I had never handled ropes and wires of that size. On reflection, I suspect that the art of seamanship is a good working knowledge of what is most unlikely to happen next.

Aft in the crowd appeared the Lamptrimmer, Bo'sun's side-kick and senior A.B. I have never heard language like his before or since. With Dutch origins, they had obviously thrown him out because he could not speak Dutch. He seemed to have joined in with the British Merchant Service to practise speaking. What he spoke was a hard, unwell-enunciated sort of fractured English which firstly nobody understood, and secondly sounded as if somebody had stuck a boat hook in your ear and started twisting it round.

Clearing the Tyne, I was stationed with an A.B. to tend the pilot ladder. Standing and waiting for the pilot to go, and still reeling from the noise, I asked the A.B. quietly about the Lamptrimmer.

'Oh, you mean Jan. Bloody fine, and he'll teach you a lot if you learn his lingo. Be careful only to listen to it, don't speak it. He's a bit catching and it would upset your folks if you went home and spoke his brand of mangled Walloon to them.'

Pilot away, in ladder and off for a quick cup of pantry tea. Jan was drawing some dry stores for the crew and he came out with the finest English effort he ever did make.

'Vor twenty years I learn how to call yam jam, and now you call it yelly.'

We were on day work, being too ignorant to be put on a watch. The big clean-up of the bridge started: ships manage to get filthy in a home port. I'd finished scrubbing the wheelhouse deck when the Second Mate appeared.

'Were you brought up in a lighthouse?'

A puzzled, 'No, Sir,' from me.

'Well scrub in the bloody corners then.'

There seemed to be a lot of glass on the bridge, what with wheelhouse front and side windows and the cabs at the wings of the bridge. The Mate had a theory that windows could be cleaned with newspaper: it never seemed to work. All we ended up with was little bits of damp paper everywhere. Ask any woman and they will agree that newspapers for windows are marvellous; seemingly after they have added to the water a drop of turps or meths, or gin, according to taste. We once caught the Mate having a practice run: it didn't work for him either, though he refused to admit it. On reflection, it must have been the salt, I suppose. A chamois leather would have saved a lot of time and annoyance at not doing a simple job fairly quickly. Chamois leathers were always kept locked in Fort Knox, the Mate's locker, because they got stolen otherwise. When I was mate, years later, one of the best tips I had was always to cut a new leather in half, because this obviously made two.

We were very glad to clear the continent and run out of newspapers; with a sideways glance of hatred from the Mate, when he found that he hadn't got the little reserve he thought he was going to have. We used Brasso after that, but it was regarded as liquid gold to use for window cleaning, although we could use plenty on the multitude of brass fittings on the bridge.

The outside brass was covered with soggy canvas covers in port: telegraphs, binnacles and so on. On leaving harbour the battle started. Wire wool, brick dust, pumice stone were all used in the fray, until the brass was 'up' enough to use Brasso. Once the brass was 'up' it was a short job each morning to keep it that way, but come the next port, back went the soggy bloody covers again.

The weather across to the Skaw was bright and clear but she was rolling enough in a northerly swell for fiddles to be fitted on the saloon tables to stop cutlery and crockery sliding off, also the tablecloths were kept wet. I was quite pleased with the motion, as I had been worried about seasickness, being prone to it in yachts and fishing vessels. Here on an ocean-going craft things were going to be alright for me. Others were less lucky.

Working on the bridge I heard the Second Mate enquire where Brown, one of his watch-keepers, was.

'Looking for Hughie, Sir.'

'What do you mean, looking for Hughie? We haven't got a Hugh aboard.'

'Well, I don't know about that, but Brown is down on the main deck and keeps leaning over the rail and shouting Hughieeeee . . .'

One of the terms for vomiting that has always stuck in my mind was 'a technicolour yawn'.

The ship was a pre-war vessel of about five thousand gross tons; five hatches, ten derricks, ten steam winches, steam reciprocating engine, three oil-fired boilers which gave her a speed of ten knots maximum. Being pre-war custom built, she was very different in several ways from many of our contemporary tramps, which were war-time built and naturally a bit schooner-rigged in the way of accommodation and non-necessities. We could lift about six thousand tons.

A crew of about forty-five, including three Mates, four Engineers, Radio Operator and the Chief Steward. Bo'sun, Chippy, Second Steward, nine A.B.s, three deck boys and three catering boys were the European complement. The engine ratings were a pleasant Arab bunch. Manning the galley were Chief Cook, Second Cook and Baker, and Galley Boy; some second cooks did bake and some didn't – there was a wage increase if they did.

The ship's crew generally was known as the Crowd, but more specifically it meant all the deck ratings. I think nearly half our European crowd were army dodgers, only to stay at sea until the age of twenty-six; they weren't too interested in much. It seemed strange to me that, to avoid eighteen months or two years National Service, these chaps would do a bored nine in the Merchant.

The A.B.s were split into three, and by doing four hours on and eight hours off, covered the six watches of the day: these six watches were known as Afternoon, Evening, First, Middle, Morning and Forenoon. The deck watch provided a wheelman only during daylight, but at night a lookout and stand-by man. The stand-by man was meant to hang about where he could be called by hand-whistle; and very often did. The lookout was kept on the fo'c's'le head, but in heavy weather was withdrawn to the Monkey Island. The Monkey Island was the deck over the wheelhouse, where the Standard Magnetic Compass was situated for a good all-round bearing view; also up there was a maritime signal mast, always referred to as the Christmas Tree. The wheelman did two hours duty and that left a man who would not be on the wheel during that particular watch; he for some reason, was known as the Farmer. So occasionally, the statement could have been made 'The Farmer was on the Monkey Island, leaning against the Christmas Tree'!

Several birds joined us on the way across; it was November and practice was to put some water and food out and leave them alone.

Rounding the Skaw put the swell astern and rolling ceased as we entered the Kattegat and made down for the Sound. There are three ways into the Baltic, all side by side: the Sound to the east, then the Great Belt, and a rather little Little Belt to the west.

We made the approach to the Sound on a brilliant Sunday

morning. By coincidence I was reading C S Forrester's *The Commodore*, in which he describes Hornblower approaching and passing the Sound. It was fascinating to have a little read and then have a little look. Forrester describes it better than I ever could. It was the first of his many Hornblower books that I had read, and ever after I always checked up on him with a chart. He did his homework faultlessly, although I feel he did cheat a very little bit when he describes Hornblower's arrival in Central America. But in that part of the world, a bit of leniency is often allowed. Go there: El Supremo's mountain is obvious, but nobody is going to walk up it every day of the week.

The birds, who didn't seem to have taken any sustenance at all, perked up one by one and flew off, and one wondered if we had taken them in the right direction. On reflection, I suspect the little beggars were just taking a ride and were not tired at all. If human females make an illicit trip, it is known as 'ringbolting', but I never did hear that term applied to birds of the feathered variety.

We passed Elsinore, where of course Hamlet had operated, without being fired on; the Swedes and Danes were obviously still neutral. The next mark after clearing the Sound was Falsterbo, and that put us properly in the Baltic.

As we approached Scandinavian waters there had been growing talk of Route Buoyage and some strange but apparently semi-splendid thing called NEMEDRI. Catching the Second Mate at a quiet moment, I asked what it was all about, and was invited to come to the chartroom at the end of his watch.

The waters of the Baltic and approaches were mined during the war. It seems that every nation joined in for defensive or offensive reasons. The areas covered by mines were too large to be swept outright, so certain channels only were swept clear. These channels were buoyed and each had a code letter. The buoys on a route were given the code letter and a consecutive number. The whole effort was contained in an Admiralty publication called *Northern Europe and Mediterranean Routing Information*, known for short as NEMEDRI.

NEMEDRI gave your buoys and their positions on a route and the width of channel, be it five or ten miles wide, or whatever. There being several ports in the Baltic, a sketch map of the routes put one in mind of a giant spider's web (drawn, alas, by a spider that had gazed too long upon the *vin blanc* when it was red). There were few clear areas. These hadn't necessarily been cleared; it usually meant somebody had forgotten to mine them originally.

So it was busy hopping around the bottom of Sweden. Very nice, one thinks, but with the odd buoy missing or its light out, and thrown in some hazy weather, the navigators were a bit preoccupied.

NEMEDRI is still in force and much used. The mines must be wearing out after all this time, but who is going to deviate and check? I'm still waiting to see a boat or a house called NEMEDRI, it would be a far less stupid name than several I've recently met with.

We had a smooth run through the lower Baltic and the Gulf of Bottina. The ship was on charter to load woodpulp in Sweden for the Argentine, and we called at Soderheim, Sundsnall and Garle, together with six other places that were referred to as ports but which turned out to be just a jetty in convenient parts of convenient fjords. Baled woodpulp was a pleasantly clean and trouble-free cargo, the only thing we had to do was mark off lots with grease crayon.

In the first port the Mate found out too late that Swedish stevedores had big pockets and also thought hatch wedges were glorious for firewood. As a result, my mate and I were sent with Chippy to saw up a new set at as furious a pace as possible.

Needless to say, the new ones were carefully guarded.

There was not much shore-going by the Crowd as they had as yet earned little money to sub.

One of the ABs managed to have a sufficiently happy time to be adrift during the working day. Then the terrible discipline enforced by the Merchant Shipping Act was put into play. He was sent for by the Old Man, and with the Mate in attendance, had his named placed in the log-book together with a note that he was fined a day's pay and forfeited another one. Should the man do the same thing again, the fine could be doubled, and doubled again for a future offence. It was not a bad system in its way. It meant that a bad hat could be hit heavily if he continued messing about. Whereas in most ships I was ever in, the man that took his initial logging as a warning and then behaved for the rest of the trip, found on pay-off day that things seemed to have been forgotten. A seaman of impossible nuisance would end the voyage with a Double DR for conduct and ability instead of the customary Very Good. DR simply meant Decline to Report on the Master's behalf. It was damning and the seaman had to do some swift talking when he went for an interview with the mate of his next ship, otherwise no job.

Should an apprentice get himself into the log-book, he would not be allowed to sit for his Second Mate's Ticket by the Board of Trade, so end of career in effect from time of logging. I only ever met one cadet who had been logged, and he, realising he was finished, sold all the eight ship's mooring ropes when he was night-watchman. He had the foresight to leave the wire back springs, otherwise the vessel might have drifted away. He also had the foresight to go ashore in the morning, otherwise physical violence would have occurred as soon as his Chief Officer found out. Eight 120-fathom, six-inch circumference ropes were a lot to sell in one night; he was a funny sort of beggar, and no doubt that was why he was logged in the first place. Thank goodness my company did not employ such people, or should I say, seemed to manage not to. The term 'money for old rope' is a misnomer; it wasn't too bad. The ship in question had to buy her own ropes back after much devious but quick negotiation, involving the customs, and agent, the Harbour Master and the Old Rope Man.

The Official Log only logged incidents of some import, otherwise there was not much in it except a list of crew and the names of the ports used, with careful departure draught particulars. On its front cover was a bold statement that the Master of a ship cannot marry people; I wonder how many passengers have had that flashed at them late at night by a tired and annoyed Old Man.

Sweden was a quiet interlude which lasted for about three weeks and the stevedores only worked days. The weather was bright and clear, but signs of ice were everywhere. The temperature at night was below freezing so, when the stevedores had left, the deck winches, windlass and warping winch were all put out of gear and set to run slowly all night, in order to keep themselves and the deck steam lines free of ice. Jan, who as nightwatchman was warned particularly to mind the hatch wedges, remarked enthusiastically, 'Ja, and I see someone stealing and I go for them lock, stock and depthcharge.'

Ice was beginning to show thinly over the fjord a couple of days before we left; nothing for us to worry about. The mate told a tale at lunch one day about an ice-strengthened ship leaving a fjord under much harsher conditions. They came across a horse and cart crossing from the starboard bow over the ice.

'Stop engines!' said the pilot.

'What!' said the Old Man, 'If you think I'm going to give way to a bloody horse and cart, you've got another think coming. Full ahead!'

It had to be tactfully put to him that if he didn't let it pass ahead, the horse and cart could hardly pass astern once the ice had a channel broken in it.

The end of loading came in Gavle, and as each of the five hatches finished, Bo'sun, Chippy, the Crowd and us cadets moved in to batten down for the passage. It would have been embarrassing for the Mate if all five hatches had finished at once, with a proper battening-down in prospect. King and Queen beams in, hatch boards on, three tarpaulins, the first under-folded to fit the hatch square – this known as tabled – the other two hauled tight over the hatch covering and placed in cleats, then battens in the cleats, and it was time for Chippy to start turning up with his precious hatch wedges, which he slammed into their position with his maul.

Derricks were lowered, and their heads securely lashed, then had their guys secured to the derrick heels. Guy ropes were coiled over the guy tackle and neatly lashed, at least where any army dodger had not been operating; I did far better than that breed: they had no interest at all. Moving ahead of Chippy and closing another hatch, we imagined we could still hear an occasional piteous cry as a manoeuvring apache wharfie managed to knock off another of his wedges.

Somebody managed to sail us at 9 o'clock on a bright morning and I think that was one of the last times that I sailed at a reasonable hour. Running south down the Gulf of Bothnia and picking up the best bit of Route buoyage to take us to Kiel, the weather changed to a cold and showery westerly. I turned to wearing brand new oilskins; by that I mean coat and a hat called a sou'wester. The term sou'wester was obviously something to do with sailing ships and south-westerly gales. They are very handy hats but very impersonal because they fit almost anybody and consequently you lose them. I am not suggesting for a moment that they were stolen. You gained one and lost one. I have always managed to lose one more than I ever gained.

Sea boots were also part of the rig and, with wet steel decks and the vessel's motion, one soon learned to walk carefully, because these conditions literally made it ideal for your feet to slide from under you. Jan kindly pointed out to me that if you turned the front lip of the sou-wester up, firstly you could see where you were going, and secondly it acted like a gutter to the back of the hat. He also explained with great delight, that it was a good idea to wear the hat outside the oilskin coat, so that all the water which collected in front did not go straight down your neck. Furthermore, it appeared *de rigeur* to wear a rope yarn lashing round the waist to stop the coat flapping about; this was known as a body and soul lashing. Of course, they fixed me up with a brand new length of one-inch rope, knowing that any newly broached gear would catch the Mate's eye. I'll never forget the contemptuous hatred he managed to put into the question. 'What's that round your waist, a body and soul lashing or a bloody tow rope?'

So away we went, making her tight for an ocean passage, and as one worked the new language of the sea emerged. Geography was vastly different. The Thames became the London River, and the Atlantic the Western Ocean. Curiously enough, I never ever heard the term 'seven seas' mentioned, I suspect because of a tacit agreement that it would have caused too much argument about which of the many seas the number seven applied to.

The only thing of note on the passage was when one of the catering boys emptied a bucket of water over the side and found out too late that there had been cutlery as well. Horrified cabin boy was not in it, because the ship's cutlery was a pleasant silver plate with the company's name and crest attached, and the Chief Steward would probably have a fit of the highest order. No doubt to give the lad confidence in his time of need, some onlookers chanted slowly, 'Tinkle, tinkle, little spoon; knife and fork will follow soon.' So much for Merchant Service sympathy. The onlookers moved gently away as, in the distance, the Chief Steward, having heard the chant, stared to make a noise like a orang-utan with its balls caught in a chandelier.

Arrival in Kiel bay was disappointing because of darkness, though an illicit look at the chart showed what a superb haven it was. Daylight was just breaking as we entered the canal lock.

The mooring operation aft had developed some sort of pattern. There were seven of us: the Second Officer, Jan, an old A.B. called Charlie, two Senior Ordinary Seamen, myself and a deck boy. It should have been a formidable team, but various circumstances interfered. There was a fairly large deckhouse, which was part of the crew accommodation on the poop, and the mooring bitts were each side of it. A steam warping winch was placed forrard of the house with extended shafts to the barrel ends, which had to be in line with fairheads and bits each side; the winch was very, very, ancient and I suspect had seen use in more than one ship, ours being the second or third.

From the top of the house out to port and starboard were built two narrow railed platforms which made a docking bridge. The Second Officer went to his station there to relay us messages from the telephone which was in the centre of the house.

The deck boy was 'Peggy', that is, taking his turn at cleaning the crew messroom and doing their washing-up. He was also a rather startled first-tripper. He used to wait until the first bit of docking action started, shout something about peggying, and disappear into the accommodation banging the door; one gone.

The two SO Seamen were both army dodgers at their most turgid. Jan used to lead one to the winch and turn the steam on, then instruct him to hold the reversing lever back. 'Saves dirtying a piece of line tying it back,' said Jan. The winch emitted such clouds of steam and noise that nobody saw or heard of the winchman again until we were all fast and Jan turned the steam off; two gone.

The second SOS army dodger was placed between numbers four and five hatches with a cork pudding fender. 'That is the best place for someone as dozy as him,' said Jan.

'Won't he drop it in the dock?'

'I tie it to his wrist!' said Jan.

'What happens if he comes aft with it and gets mixed up with the mooring lines, wires and heaving lines?'

'I don't think he do that,' said Jan, a bit absently. 'I also tied the fender line to a cleat on the bulwarks with half a dozen jamming hitches, and reckon it will be about half an hour before the bloody idiot come to cause injury on the poop. Anyway, he look more tidy there.' Three down.

The Second Officer on his docking bridge had problems. If he was on a wing seeing what was going on, the telephone rang so he had to sprint halfway across the poop to answer, and then repeat the orders given. His next move was to start shouting down to the poop deck and we couldn't hear what he was saying because of the winch noise. We didn't want to look up for hand signals as we wished to watch the lines we were operating. Anyway, by the time he'd done his dumb show once, the telephone used to ring, and away he'd dash for more orders. Four down.

This left Jan, Charlie and me to handle tug lines, stern lines, spring, heaving lines and the occasional messenger rope. I call it three hands, but I was still at the stage where I could make it two and a half, or one and a half, and Charlie had turned out to be deaf. One thing I had been taught at home on the boats was that if you don't know, get out of the way of experienced men who do, observe, and ask afterwards. Experienced seamen Jan and

Charlie certainly were. It all worked alright, but in British ships it usually does.

I was amused later in my career to be Second Mate on my own docking bridge with my own telephone. Nine times out of ten the orders were to do something we'd done and the tenth was for something we were already doing.

The same performance arose leaving the canal, and then docking and sailing from Las Palmas. On the way through the South Atlantic the after telephone went wrong, and the Third Engineer, who doubled as electrician, even after earnest consultation with the Chief, couldn't fix it. So, on future stand-bys, the Second Officer stood amongst us on deck accepting perfectly good hand signals from the bridge and passing them on; he even had time to hold the odd rope stopper. Jan found a key from somewhere and once the Peggy was on deck, used to quietly lock the deckhouse doors so this bolt hole was gone.

Five now; things were looking up. Jan still had the two dodgers out of the way, but there was the occasional chance to dive through the steam cloud shrouding the winch and alter the steam valve setting. A signal to the dodger to do so meant you got flat out or bugger all.

Kiel was a very smart lock, albeit the stone and brickwork was bomb-chipped and battered. The quay was fancily covered with square paving stones set in circular swathes; and let into these were large coloured emblems of the old Imperial Germany.

We received orders to wait in the lock for an hour. What a well-run canal we thought, because it was right on breakfast time. My mate, who was with the forrard party, had been on the cold fo'c's'le with Chippy on our run-in through Kiel Bay. He had been up there for over three hours and while changing I was able to reassure him that there were definite signs of his turning blue. I'd picked the right spot aft where there was always the lee of the deckhouse. On the fo'c's'le there was no shelter at all, and that morning there was a cold and strong WNW wind.

My mate stopped turning blue about halfway through his cornflakes, then came a nice little double act from the Old Man's table, with both he and the Mate speaking like jolly uncles.

'Ah! Mr Mate, as we go through the canal, are the cadets going to have a good view?'

'Oh! yes, Sir. I've thought of a splendid job where they will have a really lovely view of the Canal.'

The rest of the Saloon smiled at its bacon, eggs and something. I looked at my mate and we both looked at the deckhead; we knew enough of the Chief Officer's sense of humour by now to be wary.

On leaving the lock, the kindly Mate revealed his occupation for us. It was to wash the paintwork in the walkways across the fore end of the lower bridge. With the ship steaming into a head wind, it was more like trying to wash a bloody wind-tunnel out. It was the coldest day I had ever spent up to that time. My mate started turning blue again halfway through the morning; I was concerned but not worried. When I did worry was later, when I started turning blue, but my mate consolingly explained that if you were as cold as we were and didn't turn blue, there was something medically wrong with you.

Evening brought the locks of Brunsbottel, which we passed through quickly, and we turned down the Elbe for the open sea. The open sea, when reached, was still mined from war time. NEMEDRI gave two routes to the southern North Sea. The inner route was a bit crowded with traffic and, in possibly poor weather and with no radar, it was wise, but further, to take the outer route. As luck would have it, visibility stayed good until we were well through the Dover Straits. The inner route was known as the 'Route' and the outer the 'Hinder'. Both ended up off the

Dutch coast at their respectively named lightships. The inner was always reckoned to be a bit too crowded for ships without radar and in poor visibility. We took the outer route and the next day saw the Old Man and the Mates on the bridge all smiling and happy at the same time, which was most unusual. I enquired very tactfully from the Second Officer why they were so amused. He asked me to look at the weather above and around us, which was almost perfect. Then he made me look again to the south, where on the horizon was showing a cloud of what was obviously white; it was frowned upon to use the word 'fog' at sea.

The Old Man joined us. 'Yes,' he said lightly, 'the inner route's as thick as guts from the Elbe right the way through to the Tschelling light vessel. Where, on our route, we come out at the North Hinder twenty-five miles west of Tschelling, it's as clear as a bell.'

'Come into the chartroom and I'll show you,' ordered the Old Man. There it all was in radio messages – several ships anchored in the fairway and four collisions so far. It's those bastards that anchor in the fairway, they never get hit, but two other ships often collide avoiding them.' Well, well, so the Old Man could unbend at times.

'Been teaching the Master to navigate, I suppose,' my mate said. I asked him where he had been. He laughed. 'While the Old Man was talking to you, the Mate got me to one side and asked when I would turn completely non-blue again. Nothing loth, I said it should be by about tea-time, or, if I had a drop of spirits, more quickly. We went straight down to his cabin and he produced a three-quarter tumblerful of rum. Even then he said I was to regard it as medicine and not eye it, but drink it all at once. I choked, but only after the rum was safely down. I wonder if that bloody Mate will ever come out with something straightforward.'

The clear weather lasted through the straits of Dover and then turned to rain. This suited the Mate well, it seemed, and he wanted all paintwork washed or soojied. 'Sooji' was a mixture of soda and a Shell product called Teepol mixed in a bucket of hot fresh water. One of us soojied and one of us washed off with fresh water and dried. Why we dried while it was raining goodness only knows, except that was the system. The Mate had warned us that, being apprentices, we were not allowed to work more than six feet above the deck. So the watch on deck soojied the masts, Samson posts and Christmas Tree, while we started on the fo'c's'le and worked aft cleaning rails, bulwarks, mast houses, ventilators and anything else that got in the way. The Bo'sun, or 'Four Eyes' as he was known, had funny theories about the speed at which sooji-ing took place. After missing one complete morning smokoes and being knocked off late for lunch, we got the message and speeded up considerably. Four Eyes knocked us off at five o'clock and we politely asked him why we'd had no afternoon smokoe.

'This morning you didn't need one, but this afternoon, when I came to knock you off, you two were working so well and so fast that it seemed a shame to stop you.' Four Eyes, bugger him!

Four Eyes, the Boatswain, addressed as Bose. I hadn't come across him much before and, if he worked us like he had today, I didn't want to come across the split-arsed old gumshoot very much more. Next day we seemed to get the speed of work right to be knocked off for both smokoes, lunch and completely.

Seeing Four Eyes measuring out the sooji each morning was amusing in itself. He could not bear to give anything away, and although he'd flop the soda in by the handful and splash Teepol in from its drum, the mixture could not have been more accurate if he'd used a mustard spoon to dole it out.

Teepol had an interesting origin. During the war it had been found that too often survivors from a stricken vessel were safely in lifeboats but covered in oil fuel. Sitting around covered in oil fuel does not please the human body, particularly when it's wet and cold and probably suffering shock. The Shell company realised that a salt water solvent detergent was needed and developed a product, later commercially known as Teepol. This meant that with a can of the liquid provided to each lifeboat, the crew had a chance to clean up with all the ocean to use as an additive. Like all detergents the secret lay in not using too much; with Four Eyes and his mustard spoon judgement there was no chance of that in our case.

On down-channel and with rain in plenty about, the sooji continued. You didn't have to have rain, but it saved a bit on water if you did.

From what we learnt from the bridge, nothing had been seen since Dungeness, and the vessel was running on D.R, soundings and radio bearings; the last not necessarily being very accurate. D.R. stands for Deduced Reckoning, shortened into Ded'd Reckoning. It nearly always gets misspelt into Dead Reckoning; it was a plot of the vessel's time and ded'd distances on the chart.

We used to get these pieces of information from the Third Officer who had taken to dropping into our accommodation for a yarn each evening before he went on watch at eight o'clock. He remarked, à propos of something, that the fo'c's'le looked very orderly during docking stations. My mate explained the operation to me. The Chief Officer had the Bo'sun to supervise generally, and Chippy to drive the windlass, working ropes, wires, or anchors and cables. There were three A.B.s and two deck boys who had both been to sea before. There were also two army dodgers but Four Eyes was well ahead. One he placed at the jackstaff with the House Jack and orders that it should fly when the first rope was ashore, or we anchored, or vice versa if leaving anywhere. The other one he placed at the anchor ball halyards just behind the windlass with instructions to hoist it when the anchor was let go and dip it when the anchor came aweigh. In spite of all the remindful noise of anchor cable working, Chippy always had to nudge him into action. Some friction had developed between him and Chippy, because it was his habit to let the light basket-made ball down at the run. Unfortunately he had done the same thing in darkness with the brass anchor light, and it had landed on Chippy.

Chippy was rather strange-looking, and the nearest description my mate could get was that he looked somehow as if he were wearing a gas mask inside his face. Chippy apparently was reticent about the power of his windlass, his only comment being: 'A windlass is like a woman – it either will or it won't.'

The Third Mate explained that the big sooji was the start of a long process whereby the Mate would try and have the vessel spotless on return to the U.K. During the course of the voyage it would be a case of chipping, painting and scraping, bit by bit, depending on the length of time we were away. The crew were on two-year Articles of Agreement and, though nobody expected the trip to last that long, it was always at the back of the mind.

Deaf Charlie, who'd arrived to borrow something and heard the word 'woman' observed: 'A ship is like a woman, neither is ever sufficiently adorned.' Dibdin I think. Asked what else Dibdin had to say, Charlie quietly quoted:

> 'God and the sailor all alike adore
> But only when in danger note before.
> The danger over both are alike requited,
> God is forgotten and the Sailor slighted.'

The Third Mate and Charlie gone, we fell to discussing our shipmates; there was obviously far more in them than met the eye. Word had it that Chippy had been in a German P.O.W. camp for five years and that one of the A.B.s, Hank, also getting on in years, had only one interest and that was horse-racing, certainly a queer hobby for a seaman. The Fourth Engineering Officer was apparently a keen ballroom dancer; the Third Engineer Officer's wife kept Pekingeses; the elderly Radio Officer was a Yoga enthusiast: with this last my mate unkindly remarked that the dear old fellow could well have invented it.

The rain and muck continued until we were about 35°N, that is roughly level with Gibraltar. Then one morning there was bright sunshine and an almost clear blue sky. It was surprising the difference it made, everybody had an extra smile or an extra stupid remark to spare; overnight the ship had changed from something sombre to something cheerful, and so she remained.

That evening the Third Mate told us that the morning sun sights had given a position which was only three miles different from the D.R., which after several days running blind had pleased the bridge staff no end. No adjustment of the course was needed to make Las Palmas, where we were to take bunker oil. Shipowners always look for the cheapest bunkers available during voyages, and the subject is quite an important one in the Charter Party, that is, the agreement between us and our Charterers. Sea lore has it that in olden days the hiring agreement was written out twice, side by side on the same sheet of paper and signed and sealed twice; the charter or writing was then torn in half, or parties, so both hirers and owners had identical sets and in case of argument the first thing to do was to see if the two papers fitted at the tearing line. This was standard legal procedure until comparatively recent times. Usually the two documents were clipped with notches on their edges – indented. Therefore they were called 'Indentures', e.g. 'Indentures of Apprenticeship'.

Gran Canaria was sighted many miles away one morning and

we arrived at lunchtime; ships very, very often sail, arrive or shift during the period that would have been a meal hour. Then running down off the breakwater, which was well over a mile long, we started seeing what ships were in. Two passenger liners, one Royal Mail returning from the Plate, and one Union Castle outward-bound for the Cape; four or five tramps, and a tanker alongside, left just one berth for the pilot to guide us to.

The berth was oil-sodden and the water near it was black on top. Nothing unusual about a bit of pollution in those days. First aboard was a party consisting of the ship's Agents, Customs and Health officials who went straight up to the Old Man's cabin. About ten minutes later the Third Officer came aft shouting for 'Q' flag to be hauled down and 'P' to replace it.

'Q' flag was yellow and its meaning 'My vessel is healthy and I request free *pratique*.' Lowering the flag meant *pratique* was granted, and was the signal for a small stream of people to mount the gangway: an oil company representative to see the Chief Engineer about the bunkers and a little man in a large black beret, who went into a huddle with Chippy and the Mate about taking on fresh water, were the most important arrivals. The Ship Chandler made a line for the Chief Steward's cabin, particularly looking for a fresh vegetable order. The Scrap Brass Man sought out the Second Engineer, followed by the Bo'sun remarking to us, 'The daft bastard doesn't seem to have realised that there is no scrap brass on tramp ships, or if there is it is still in use.' He was followed by the Old Rope Man asking to see the Mate, and the Bo'sun this time shrugged and said, 'He's wasting his time too, our ropes are too old even for him, and he can see that from the dock.' Next up was the shore watchman who had the low-down on sailing time, which would be seven o'clock that evening. He was followed by four people carrying large suitcases, who were the Bumboat. In ports around the world people like to sell stuff to seamen, from up-town emporia to dilapidated shops just outside dock gates. The people who really closed in for business were the ones that brought it to the ship, by boat or by car. These were traditionally known as bumboatmen and had a Chief Bumboatman in charge. The suitcases were opened and their contents displayed on the edge of number four hatch, market-stall fashion. Cigars, fans, shawls, lighters, dolls, and of course canaries in birdcages. Some of the crew bought canaries and pleasant little pets they turned out to be. The Bumboat had a beguiling feature: we did not have to pay cash, just to sign. The Chief Bumboatman would take the list to the Old Man to receive payment shortly before the vessel sailed.

My mate and I were told to relieve each other as gangway watchman, and also to rig the sailing board with 'No Shore Leave' in a prominent position. The duties were to stop any of the crew going ashore, even for just a little walk on the quay, and to stop drink coming aboard. This last was rather a failure because we afterwards found that the Bumboatmen had been smuggling it aboard bottle by bottle and letting the crew sign for it as something else. The brew was known to seamen as Las Palmas brandy, though if it was actually made there I never discovered.

So it was a five-hour stretch, with some of the crowd gathered round the Bumboat and the head of the gangway, chatting and watching the traffic to and from the passenger boats. The highlight was four drunken seamen, with the drink visibly taking effect on them, as they staggered slowly past us to collapse at the bottom of their own very long gangway; not a good advertisement for the passengers. Their Chief Officer acted quickly and had them slung aboard in a cargo net which I always felt was the height of indignity, but in the circumstances justified. Old Sparkie appeared and said that he had to go over to the British tanker that was in to check on some publication; not our business to stop an officer on business.

One of the deck boys happened to enquire generally, 'How do you tell whores?'

'No drawers!' was the loud reply from his listeners.

Sparkie at the gangway turned and looked the boy sternly up and down. 'When you get to my age you will find a good stiff shit is as good as a woman any day,' and went on his way amidst howls of laughter.

Jan had been chatting to a bumboatman he knew and came across smiling about a riddle he'd just heard. We were obviously in for it. Jan's normal language was atrocious; how would he get a riddle over? It took a quarter of an hour to get it over. 'If the lifespan of man is from the womb to the tomb, what is the lifespan of an egg?' Jan was in such a state of mirth that getting the answer was difficult. It turned out to be 'Arsehole to breakfast time'.

The Third Officer from another tramp came to ask if we would exchange ship's libraries, but our own Third refused, saying that we were only about a month out and our books still well used. A barber came on board, but got no trade as Hank carried some gear with him and would always provide a trim.

The Union Castle mail boat left, with passengers lining the decks. Painted a greyish pink overside, she looked very smart.

Sparkie returned from the tanker with his breath lightly spiced with something that had more to do with Scotland than radio publications. The tanker had been out for fourteen months and no sign of her going home, he reported.

The bunkering party started to take a very close interest in their work and a few minutes later a shout marked the end of bunkering and the pipe started being unbolted.

It was noticeable by now that some of the crew had taken more drink than the regulation two bottles of beer per man per day.

It was time for our flags and lights shortly before sailing. Jack, Spanish Courtesy Ensign, House Flag and Ensign. My mate covered forrard and I aft. The House flag was flown at the main masthead, in our case the after mast, and it was flown on a twelve-foot bamboo pole to keep it clear of the masthead. Hoisting the bloody thing was usually a nuisance. Flag, both ends of pole and in fact three parts of the halyard all continued to get mixed up with mainmast and two mast stays, the jumper stay and main aerial, the mainmast light being the last hurdle. Lowering was different: on a quiet night I had found it would run down quite happily on its own while I made a dash for the Ensign. This time the post near-missed Chippy with a crash, but luckily his unfortunate army dodger was passing and bore the full brunt of his wrath. 'P' flag was left flying as it indicated that the ship was sailing within twenty-four hours, and to take it down before the last mooring rope hit the water might have given some amongst us cause to plead confusion as they made for the shore.

'P' had another meaning at sea: 'Your lights are out or burning badly'. The vessel you wanted to contact obviously would not see a flag, so the letter was flashed by Morse lamp.

We sailed at half-past seven and the Third Mate called on us when he left the bridge.

'The Old Man and the Mate are going spare on the bridge, saying you two have let bottles aboard. Don't worry too much, cadets have always stood watchmen since Las Palmas, ships, gangways and bottles were invented, and always drink gets aboard. Drink used to get past me as a cadet and I'm bloody sure it used to get past the Mate when he was serving his time. Anyway, its the Old Man's fault for allowing a Bumboat at all, but he gets a ten per cent cut on the takings, so it's sans fairy snatch block,' the Third Mate ended, lapsing into a bit of Jan.

Deaf Charlie dropped by to borrow something. We had been

given strict instructions not to allow ratings of any department into our accommodation, but he seemed to be excepted from the rule, probably due to his age and deafness.

Charlie wasn't very pleased over the drink that was about, neither was the Third Mate; they'd seen it all before. The two bottles of beer issued daily were not really much use, they said. Consequently, as soon as a port was hit, so was the local grog; particularly, as in this case, when there was no shore leave. Brandy, they opined, was not too bad, but when crowds started pouring anis or tequila down themselves into completely unused systems, the results were pathetic. No, the argument was for plenty of good UK beer that could be bought on board, then everybody could take a happy drink regularly and within their capacity; local plonk would be left alone.

Darkness covers a lot of things, and the less anybody asked the less had to be answered. When I went up to the bridge at 0630 for the Mate's daily orders there was a man on the wheel and the wake was fairly straight. The orders were to clean round the bridge thoroughly, it being surprisingly dirty after a few hours in port.

All of those who started operating at 0700 or 0800 hours turned out but there were some sorry states visible, creeping around the deck for the rest of the day. One of the catering boys nearly didn't make it. The Chief Steward, with a fatherly smile, placed a galvanized bucket over the boy's head and beat it with a short piece of broom handle, known as a dhobi stick. The boy turned out; he still looked cross-eyed at lunchtime, but we didn't have the heart to ask him if he'd thanked the Chief Steward for the help.

The only casualty was a rather heavy, plump deck boy. Somebody had pinched his bedding for laughs and he turned in, or had been turned in, wearing only underpants, directly onto his bunk springs. A light sleeper, he caught odd pinches of skin in the springs each time he turned over, and by morning he looked as if a medieval torturer had been at him.

The day wore quietly away with nobody saying very much, and when darkness came peace and quiet reigned. At about 2230 I was just going off to sleep when a horrible and continuing cry rent the night. The whistle went for the standby man, and by the number of footsteps dashing to the bridge several curious people had gone to see. Our whistle signal was three blasts, so we stayed where we were.

The tale emerged the next day. The Third Mate, being caught short, had opened a panel in the starboard side light box to relieve himself overside. The Old Man, in night attire, was taking a last breath of air, leaning over the rail directly below. The Third Mate piddled all over him; the really funny part was that the Old Man didn't realise what was happening until he was fairly soaked, hence the furious noise. Why the devil the Third Mate didn't use the bridge fire bucket, like the other two Mates in time of stress, was a question we never liked to ask him.

The first fine Saturday afternoon brought a full-scale boat and fire drill; there had only been a couple of musters previously to check men as to their jobs.

At half-past four the alarm rang and started a stream of men toward the boat deck, donning lifejackets as they came. Standing in line before their respective boats everybody was again checked out on which job to do, both at boat and fire drill. I was in the Second Officer's boat and his next move was to come down the line inspecting our lifejackets. The lifejackets were in good order, but he didn't like the manner of their wearing; out of twenty-three only Jan and Charlie were in order.

'It's no use sticking these jackets over your head and tying the tapes as if you were going to the Whores' Ball. The tapes are not for decoration, they are there to keep the jacket from sliding over your head in the water and must therefore be tight. Yes, tighten the tapes until you feel uncomfortable, then you are about right. Surplus tape, wrap round your waist on its own part. Stuff it up your arse if you like, but don't have loops or bights about that can get caught in anything, because if you do they will.'

Port and starboard boats were swung out, and with the old-fashioned radial divots it was quite easy for an unwary soul to be crushed. After the boats were in, fire parties went into action, but the action usually meant looking at their particular job and explaining it to each other. The big thing was to start the emergency fire pump, placed in the steering flat to be independent of engine room fires, and have it supply a good jet via the deck line to the hose. It was quite funny on the odd occasion that someone hadn't got the nozzle properly on before water started arriving!

The other piece of gear that was tried out was the smoke helmet. This was a glass-fronted leather helmet with a sixty-foot air-line leading to a pair of bellows. I was in this party and smelled a rat as soon as ordered to don the helmet; my mate and I were beginning to develop that sixth sense a seaman requires to tell him when any leg-pull was going on.

The glass doors in the faceplate were clipped up more tightly than usual and the neck cord for the helmet's leather skirt had far more, and tighter, knots than usual. Both these facts I was about to discover.

Once I was properly fitted, others in the team operated the bellows to send a flow of air through to the helmet. Then members of the onlooking group began farting into the bellows one by one. I didn't mind if I saw a burst of laughter – that meant a good loud noise passing. To the uninitiated, raucous ones don't smell, it's the silent ones that really pervade (silent but deadly, or SBDs). It was now very unpleasant in the helmet, but with the cord snarled and the windows jammed there wasn't much I could do.

Then Hank crouched over the bellows and I could see no laughter at his effort. When it arrived it was horrible; he must have been eating wet cow cake and garlic for about a week to get himself a right rotten set of guts, the dirty bastard. I was beginning to reel a bit so they let me out. The first person I really noted was my mate who was curled up on the hatch with laughter. He would have warned me had he known and no doubt I would witness him getting something amusing, amusing that is to onlookers, later.

Strangely enough it was only until the next fire drill that I had to wait to get back at Hank. There he was, trussed immobile in the Neil Robertson stretcher, with his arms lashed across his front. Well, well, well, was he ticklish in the ribs? He was, and I gave him a bloody good dose, being careful not to overdo it, and of course had plenty of time to make a good escape while he was being undone.

'Crew exercised at Boat and Fire Drill' went into the Official Log.

Sunday mornings at sea were the time of the Old Man's weekly inspection. 'Master's Inspection of Crew Accommodation and Storerooms' was another one of the four entries made in the Official Log. Everywhere was usually pretty clean and tidy, but at 1100 Sunday everywhere had to be extra so. The Master, Chief Officer, Chief Engineer and Chief Steward appeared in full uniform and slowly went the rounds. Our part in it was negligible; we used to strew our correspondence courses around the day cabin and pretend to be so engrossed that we hardly heard the party arrive. Then they seemed to wish to disturb us as little as possible.

The galley was their next visit, where the Old Man would always ask formally for permission to enter; 'May I come in, Doc?' The answer was always 'Yes', and the galley always spotless. The spotlessness was achieved by loading up one of the cabin boys with last-minute bits that weren't and sending him off round the block with them. 'Doc' was the name for the Chief Cook in any normal ship, coming through from the not-so-distant days when the cook would doctor any livestock carried aboard for consumption.

The correspondence course was rather a nuisance; being on day work meant each evening, and Saturday afternoon and Sundays were free of ship's work, so there was no excuse for not keeping up with it. The difficult bits meant a trip to the bridge to ask the Officer of the Watch, and by alternating myself and my mate between three officers, we got a fair amount on paper without too much effort. We had to be a bit careful with the Chief Officer, as he had forgotten a lot of the elementary stuff we were on, and it would have been tactless to ask questions in the wrong field. He did like doing Ship Construction questions and I think he'd done our year's supply in about two months. Apart from the course, the three officers were most instructive in all sorts of large and small matters; no set time, but a word or two as we were working, or something happened.

One Saturday afternoon at three o'clock (six bells, Afternoon Watch) when I went for a mug of tea, I suddenly realised that I had not seen my mate since lunchtime. A general enquiry elucidated the fact that the Mate had sent him on an errand right after lunch, but I noticed one or two turned away and suppressed smiles. After a reasonably short hunt I found him in the boiler room. He explained that he'd been sent by the Mate to the Chief Engineer, and passed on by the Second Engineer to the watch-keeping Third Engineer; he was to ask for a Long Stand. By the time I'd found him he'd had a nice long stand in the boiler room for about two and a half hours and his clothes were dripping perspiration. On the way up and on meeting the Third, all he got was, 'Did you enjoy your long stand?'

Four o'clock came and three blasts on the hand whistle; my mate made a line for the bridge. The Mate was there, also the relieved Second Officer and the Master, ears aflap.

'Did you get the long stand?'

'Yes, Sir, two and a half hours in the Boiler Room.'

The Mate grinned. 'That was a bit lengthy, but I did want to make quite sure you were warm enough after the Kiel Canal weather.'

The next morning, Sunday, I was sent by the Third Mate to ask for the prayer books from the Old Man. Yes, I fell for it: from Chief Steward to Chief Officer and so on, all the way round the ship. When I did find their supposed location, the cupboard was locked. I had to retrace my steps asking for a mythical bloody key. I gave up when I met my mate who had just been sent to the Chief Engineer to ask for 'steam on the organ'. The Chief had burst out laughing and explained that it wasn't usual to have a church service in a tramp ship; this was after he had passed me on once for prayer books and twice for mythical bloody keys, the rotten bastard.

Nobody was clear of risk. One morning the Mate told Chippy to report to the Old Man, who wanted the rubber in one of his portholes renewing. Chippy came out muttering; it appeared that the Old Man wanted to do the job himself, but needed Chippy's gear to do it.

The Old Man went down to number three hatch, which was obviously to be the scene of operations and received port rubber, rubber glue and a large screwdriver, a small iron bar and a two-pound hammer from a stormy-faced Chippy. We were working near enough to see the performance and others seemed to find jobs just at corners; the catering staff sidled into the galley which had three large open ports looking forrard. Word had gone round that Chippy had a scheme afoot, but what?

The Old Man nipped the old port rubber out and threw it over the wall, then started squeezing and stretching the new stuff into place. It didn't appear to be his morning, as he utilised the large screwdriver, the small iron bar and the two-pound hammer with no success at all; by now he was standing on the hatch so he could use one of his feet as well as two hands. Finally, getting annoyed, he started battering the rubber with the hammer. Something slipped, and there was a most satisfactory crash as he put the hammer through the port glass. Throwing the hammer down he stormed off to his cabin and sent for the Mate. Shortly afterwards a satisfied-looking Chippy cleared all the gear from number three hatch and disappeared forrard to his own precincts.

It wasn't long before the port with new glass and rubber was returned to the Old Man's cabin. Chippy almost lost his gas-mask look for the rest of the day, with pleasure.

Deaf Charlie told us that evening what the trick had been: Chippy had reckoned that if he put glass, hammer, rubber and infuriated Old Man together, the glass was bound to go eventually; so he had provided the rubber a size too big, just to help things along.

Nobody had to meet the Old Man's gaze for a couple of days, or there would be something wrong about something. The end of the dark mood came with a blast at us for working without shirts. I made a line for the bridge ladder and my mate kept working. Another blast from the Old Man, until my mate explained that I had gone for both shirts. This seemed to please him no end: first trip cadets thinking about time and motion. Time and Motion wasn't in it really; the Mate had another expression, 'the quick or the dead'.

The Old Man started on about the dangers of the sun, particularly to us two, who were not used to it.

'Wait until you are working where there is no breeze and take your shirts off; you'll put them back fairly soon! While we are in the Trades, on the Doldrums or the SE Trades I don't want you lads without shirts for more than an hour a day.'

We had looked a bit blank at this mention of Trades; also the Mate appeared on the bridge to find out why he couldn't hear us working.

'Come into the chartroom and I'll show you these winds.' He was knocking us off in sacred working hours, which didn't please the Mate, and when we reached the chartroom he arrested the Second Officers' chart, which didn't please in that quarter either.

'The NE Trades blow in an area from about Las Palmas to about five degrees north of the equator. After that we'll have the calm of the Doldrums down to the Brazilian coast, then the SE Trades may touch us, but this time of year there are more likely to be NE winds on the South American coast.'

'Don't hurricanes start in the Doldrums?' asked my mate brightly.

'Yes, they start, but much further west of our bit, and they are not reckoned on as hurricanes until they gain force and approach the West Indies, and that's at a certain season:

> June too soon,
> July, stand by,
> August, look out
> September, remember,
> October all over.

Although they cause a great deal of damage ashore, a ship can usually avoid them if a careful watch is kept on the weather, because the centre is comparatively slow-moving.

'The weather I have to watch for is a *pampero*. There is no sea room and it can start to empty the estuary, blowing from the west as it does. If you're halfway up or down the narrow channel it could be a bastard.'

Five bells struck to mark ten-thirty and coffee time. The Old Man made off, giving Sparkie a healthy bollocking on the way for spilling Brasso on the wooden deck. That was five of us he'd upset in about forty minutes; good going, and he was humming happily to himself when the Second Steward took his coffee up.

Custom decreed that there was as little noise as possible between midday and fifteen-thirty; this was to enable those keeping watch to get some secondary sleep in. Our chipping and scraping was suspended at lunchtime and a less noisy activity was given us. These jobs varied early in the passage, but once into the fine weather the Third Mate, as Lifeboat Officer, decided to check the boats out. There were two reasons for this. The first was that he was paid overtime for the afternoons and the second was to sit in the sun with his clipboard directing our operations.

There were four lifeboats to check, clean and overhaul the equipment they had. Masts, sails and their rigging, the oars and rowlocks, rudder, painters and sea anchor were the main items, but there were many other small ones.

A pump was in each boat and also two galvanized buckets which were not necessarily used for baling. The oil lamp for the boat had to fit into the buckets; the idea was that a Morse message could be sent by moving the lighted lamp in and out of the bucket. An axe to chop any fouled lines was provided forrard and aft; once the boat was clear of the ship the officer was supposed to ask for the forrard axe to be passed aft, just in case anybody got any ideas of mutiny. Compass, flares and first aid were more items. Each boat was to take a stated number of people and provided for each were one pound of biscuits, one pound of barley sugar, one pound of condensed milk and three quarts of fresh water. Not much food or water, but the idea was to get an SOS away by radio, and then stay in the area of the foundering until searching vessels arrived. Given time, the boats would be stuffed with extra stores and their endurance greatly increased.

This had been the case with the *Trevassa*, which sank off the beaten track, and two boats made Rodriguez and Mauritius Islands respectively twenty-three days later. This had been in peace-time with about an hour's notice to get off the ship. The passages made by the boats were truly remarkable, being just under two thousand miles. Years later I was in Mauritius and saw a section of a museum that had been put aside for the relics of the boat voyage. Alas, the boat herself had gone. During the Second World War a damaged ship had called in and amongst other things needed a lifeboat, so the *Trevassa* boat was put back into service, and she never returned.

There was a portable radio transmitter, which would go into the Old Man's boat, together with Sparks. There were also one or two extra items that were not Board or Trade required. One of these was a set of fishing hooks. I asked my mate what he thought the fish would like for bait: biscuits, milk or barley sugar. I received a painful blow on the crown of the head from the corner of the Third Mate's plywood clipboard, and was told to get on with it all.

Going through four lifeboats took many days, because by the end of each afternoon everything had to be put back in place in case of emergency during nightfall.

One of the boats had a motor and therefore did not have to have a sail. It did, however, have to have two boathooks, the logic of this escaped me, but I dared not ask the Third Mate in case I got belted with his clipboard again.

'Crossing the line' was the term used for crossing the Equator and entering the southern hemisphere. This was the domain of King Neptune and he always liked to be greeted by clean-shaven people who were crossing for the first time. So, in every ship that passed over, a small ceremony was held, elaborate in passenger liners, simple in other ships, depending on what was available.

Curiously enough, my mate and myself, who were usually the butts of any mischief going, got clean away with it. From first coming aboard we'd made passing references to imaginary trips from Australia and South Africa made as young kids with our parents. By the time we reached the Line everybody seemed satisfied that we were in the clear as far as any frolics might go. After tea on the Day my mate sat brazenly in the cabin pretending to do his correspondence course; I took a book and a torch and hid down a cargo ventilator for an hour or so, until I was quite sure our ruse had worked.

Deaf Charlie acted as Neptune and there could obviously be no appeal there, with Chippy as a sort of admirer. Hank and Jan were in charge of the Bears, whose job it was to seek out and bring before Neptune all newcomers to his realm. The ceremony consisted of sitting each one in turn on a box in front of Neptune and shaving them with a piece of dunnage which did duty as a king-size razor. Lather was provided with a bucket, together with a whitewash brush to put it on with. The object was inadvertently to get as much soap into the victim's mouth as possible, holding the nose if necessary. The shave was a rough affair, followed by a blast of hose water in the face to wash it off. The last part was to stand the venturer under an awning spar with his hands tied up over it and paint him in stripes with quick-drying flat white paint. Chippie's unfortunate army dodger kicked somebody while being painted and ended up with his hair full of paint; he eventually had to go and ask Hank to cut the lot off.

Seamen or travellers in a liner company usually got a certificate signed in King Neptune's name to prove that they had been initiated.

Food was plentiful. Early morning tea from the Officers' Pantry was collected from the deck entrance. A pint of it, and arguments about sugar and milk with the cabin boys. There were two types of milk at sea, 'Connie Onnie' and 'Shaky'. Shaky was tinned evaporated and Connie Onnie was tinned sweetened condensed. Connie Onnie would have been alright in the tea with a spoonful of sugar, but there could be dispute with the cabin boys. This bunch, three of them, reckoned that Connie Onnie sweetened tea sufficiently on its own, amidst shouts of how they'd been kicked off to school on nothing else, and so on.

Shaky milk was guarded like emerald dust by the Second Steward until it had been well over-watered, 'bashed' was the technical term. So, if one asked for a pint of Shaky milk tea, dispute arose again over how many teaspoons of sugar. They'd all been sent off to school with only two, and so on. We felt three were vital, four preferable, and five ideal if we could get them. This pettiness rather annoyed us as they were not giving their mother's sugar away. Curiously enough, both of us, on comparing notes, would have preferred a glass of hot water. However, we were first-trip cadets and seamen had tea in the morning: we conformed, we had tea.

My mate developed the happy solution. One of us would ask for Shaky and the other for Connie Onnie. He would argue which was which, with plentiful quiet comments about what they did not seem to have learned at school, and the boys created uproar in no time. Once I got the message and joined in we reckoned the uproar could be nearly doubled.

The Chief Steward lived next to the pantry, and the row started waking him each morning. He enquired of the Second Steward why the cabin boys were making so much noise, and decreed that it should stop. Next morning our jibes drove the boys to a frenzy which woke the Second Mate. The Second Mate, who had come off the bridge at 0400 after keeping the Middle Watch, used to sleep until 0830 and take a late breakfast. Only a mild complaint from him to the Chief Steward that he, the Second Mate, had been woken by noise from the pantry, was enough for the Chief Steward to hold his own enquiry. We were for some reason asked to be present. The resulting deal was for one spoonful of sugar with Connie Onnie, or three for Shaky. The Sugar War was over, we thought.

Next morning heaped spoonfuls of sugar were in evidence. Quiet comments from us about this, and the noise from the boys woke the Chief Steward. They were playing the old catering staff trick of trying to substitute an eggspoon for a teaspoon. The Chief Steward arrived with a towel round him, furious. Great politeness from us: bland, thick innocence was not in it. The Sugar War was in abeyance.

Uniform in the Saloon for meals was obligatory. Blue Reefer brassbound jackets, and trousers to match. Hot weather brought out uniform khaki or white shirts and shorts. The more senior the rank, the more whites used to show. Gold braid on reefer jacket sleeves or shirt shoulder straps showed rank. Four straight stripes for the Master and Chief Engineering Officer, reducing rank by rank until the Third Mate and Fourth Engineer had one. A diamond was worked into the stripes to denote the holding of a Board of Trade Ticket. The Engineering Department had purple backing to braid. Apprentices wore lapel patches, with blues, known as Georgettes, or a plain blue shoulder strap with whites or khakis.

There were two tables which would seat eight each. The Old

Man, the Chief, the Second and the Mate sat at one, and the other seven of us at the second. The Steward had his work cut out to get round quickly when all eleven sat down together: this would be in port.

Breakfast consisted of porridge in cold weather, or cornflakes; bacon, egg and something such as sausage, tomato, hot cake, black pudding or rice cake. Then as much bread, butter and marmalade as was required to top off with. Curiously enough, the boys never tried to be tight with butter, and they had every chance to be, as we two sat stuffing after the officers had left.

Getting into the hot weather, curry and rice were served three or four days a week, instead of bacon, egg and something. To the uninitiated, curry for breakfast may seem a bit unpalatable, but once one got used to the idea, it was very splendid.

Mid-morning coffee, apart from rumblings of the Sugar War, was disgusting. It was Board of Trade approved, with their maximum amount of chicory percentage, and it came in seven-pound tins. It was obviously meant to be percolated, or nurtured at least some way other than being chucked into a steam geyser and boiled. Then it was just allowed to go hot and cold, until somebody reckoned the non-concoction was getting a bit too thin and dumped some more coffee in it. The brew produced some muddy water, which seemed to pretend it had come from the River Amazon, and about one-fifth of a mug of near-perfect coffee grains.

Lunch started with a good soup, yellow split peas was the favourite, and went on to a roast, or fish on Fridays; one vegetable and roast and boiled potatoes. Catering staffs seem to have a thing about baked and boiled potatoes, and none of them could tell you why you didn't get boiled one day and roast the next. I think Noah must have had roast and boiled potatoes and the habit stuck. Sweets were simply milk puddings, three days a week, something else for two days and duff on Wednesdays and Sundays. In those days a Chief Cook could be a bit ordinary, but if he made a really good duff it was always held in great mitigation. Bread, butter and cheese, coffee until you realised it was always going to be like this.

A mug of tea in the afternoon at the pantry door went down well. The boys, however, went berserk with the amount of tea, seemingly on the assumption that if four spoonfuls made a good cup of tea, eight would make it twice as nice.

High Tea at half-past five consisted of an entree: scrambled egg, sardines, or something. The main dish was a grill, a chop, fish, hot pot, stew, shepherd's pie-type effort; plenty of it. Sweets were provided and prunes used to appear frequently. Cold meat and salad was available, though salad gave way to pickles when the vegetables started running short. Water was often drunk with meals, but I was interested that nobody ever poured themselves a full glass; just a third of a half and a top-up if required. Shades of water rationing were with us always, it appeared.

The Galley was operated by a team of three, and had the biggest coal range that I had ever seen; albeit I had seen several large ones in country houses. I was to find these coke ranges a standard pattern for most ships of the day. I never have really understood why the cooks cursed them from morning until nightfall, and later if they could find anybody to listen. If, on the other hand, a woman saw these stoves while being shown around ship, they straightaway made coos of delight and you could see them almost looking for an apron, particularly when they were told coke was unlimited.

A cup of cocoa later in the evening ended the day, but it depended on catching the Second Steward when he opened the pantry to make the Old Man's supper tray at about eight o'clock. The tray, I noted, included a small jug of unbashed Shaky: rank had its privileges. As soon as the Second's back was turned, I used to put about half a tin of Connie Onnie into my cocoa; the one properly sweetened drink of the day!

As we steamed quietly on through the South Atlantic a disaster occurred. The Chief Steward decided to clear some odd store rooms out and in amongst a pile of junk was found a large wooden box, heavily bolted, strapped and nailed. Chippy was sent for and arrived with his demolition tools. The box opened to reveal its secret; desiccated coconut. After that we had coconut with everything. Sometimes you could see it and sometimes you couldn't, but the damn taste was always there.

Later on in my apprenticeship I was caught on a particularly non-alcoholic ship. I was reduced to buying coconuts, drilling holes in them, topping them up with sugar and plugging the hole with cement. These left to ferment gave variable results at the high end of the scale. Apart from this alcoholic help, I have never touched coco-bloody-nuts again.

Our menu cards were typed out by the Chief Steward on an ancient and battered typewriter which had several of the letters worn. This could lead to some odd meal advertising. One time I remember was when rissoles were served. As the tail of the typewriter's 'R' was gone, the Third Engineer smilingly requested, 'Pissoles, please.'

The Steward, falling into the trap, said, 'Excuse me, Third, but that is not a P, it is an R.'

The Third jumped in, 'Arseholds, then, please, Steward.' Roars of laughter all round, but we never got rissoles again. Bad language was hardly ever used at tables, but everybody agreed that that opportunity had been too good to miss.

Tales were told of other ships' and Companies' feeding, some good some bad. But the prize for the most tight-fisted outfit went to a certain liner company who, on their intermediate ships, required the officers to sit at the heads of tables in the passenger saloon. The menus presented at table had an asterisk placed beside anything slightly exotic; this told the Officer that he was not allowed to order the dish.

The occasional other tale would bring the rebuke from the Old Man sitting in pomp at the head of his table: 'Mister . . . save that sort of talk for your smokeroom, I do not want it in my saloon.'

We all agreed that he was more than justified when the Third Engineer was speaking about his time in a troopship.

'I was working in the lift shaft one day when she was rolling too much to have the ancient lifts working. Up the deserted stairway came a soldier carrying a large dixie of porridge. Suddenly he turned green and heaved up straight into the dixie; reaching the next deck he found room to stand the dixie safely down, rolled his sleeve up and hurriedly gave the mixture a good stir.'

Conversation at table was always of interest and could cover anything. All the officers were married except the Third Officer, but the subject of marriage was touched on but not dwelt on. The big impression I had from them was that the best wife for a seaman was another seaman's daughter because she would have learned from her mother the drawbacks and ins and outs of marrying near salt water. The only problem was that no seaman in his right mind would let another seaman anywhere near his daughter.

Birds at sea seemed to have no significance to anybody. We'd picked up the usual albatross, which I was told would stay with us for the remainder of the ocean passage. The bird never deviated from its gentle flight, except when the galley gash bin was emptied over the wall. They apparently slept on the wing, but stayed further from the ship than in daylight; people had tried looking for them with the narrow-beamed Aldiss signal lamp at night but had no luck. Everybody knew the albatross because of its size; if it had flown backwards for a day I doubt if anybody would have remarked on the fact, assuming they had noticed.

The bo'sun bird was a bit larger than the run of the ocean birds and had a flat-ended diminishingly thin tail which nearly came to a point before entering the body. On asking why it was called a bo'sun bird, Deaf Charlie told me it was because its call resembled that of a Royal Naval bo'suns pipe whistling.

Jan said, 'It's because it has a marlin spike stuffed up its arse.'

Every other bird, no matter what its shape, colour, speed, breed or creed, was simply known as a Shitehawk.

I got used to seeing passing ships not far off our own course line and bound to or from the Plate. Many were tramps like ourselves, and nearly all of these wartime built. I mistakenly used the phrase 'liberty ship' to the Chief Engineer and he expanded on the subject.

'Wartime built vessels referred to *en masse* are known as liberty ships, but if you are referring to one ship you should get used to recognising and referring to the type. Three countries built them: UK, Canada and USA. We called all our ships "Empire something". The Canadians built two standard vessels, the Fort and Park boats; that is "Fort Something" or "Something Park", which were handed over the UK for crewing in most cases. The Americans built "Ocean" ships for British ownership, but their own two most popular ones were called the "Something Victory" or "Sam Something", Sam being after Uncle Sam. The "Victories" were large, fast and turbine driven, whereas the "Sams" were tramp size and speed. The "Sams" had a bad name for breaking in two in mid-Atlantic, but only one sank with loss of crew; at one stage of the war it seemed as if you could hardly get into a UK port for towed-in stern halves of Sam boats. Their basic design was done on the Clyde, so nobody could really laugh on either side of the Atlantic. However, several bow sections were towed in as well and it was more or less a case of welding the nearest bow to the nearest stern half, strengthening her a little, and you had a bloody good ship. I know, I spent a year in one; the only real trouble then was that we ended up with administrative mail for two ships instead of a single bastard. We got round that by keeping the easy letters and sending the difficult ones off to the Sam Boat which was the stern to our bow section.'

One morning, brass polishing, I noted that the Third Officer was taking a lot of interest in a very distant vessel, almost right astern. The Old Man, from wherever he was, also noted the Third's behaviour and came up to the bridge. The names *Alcantara* and *Andes* were frequently mentioned, but I did not understand how they would tell a ship at that distance. The overtaking vessel turned out to be *Alcantara* of the Royal Mail Line, and its accompanying albatross had to fly a bit faster than ours to keep up. On enquiring of the Third about the recognition of her, he explained that the two passenger ships which ran the liner service to the Plate were the *Alcantara* and the *Andes* and they sailed on strict schedule; it just had to be one or the other.

The whole pattern of British passenger traffic began to make itself clear. Those were the days before air travel was at all general and if anybody went anywhere they went by ship. Passenger liner schedules were known months ahead, so people picked their time and left; just like a railway system, the big difference being that, unlike trains, if you missed your ship you had a bloody long wait for the next one.

South America was served on the east coast by the two passenger ships just mentioned. It also had passenger service from intermediate lines, that was more cargo, fewer passengers, and maybe not so speedy, run by Blue Star Line and the Nelson Line which was owned by Royal Mail. Various cargo liners carried twelve passengers, but as it was the cargo that had to be on schedule, many people preferred the relaxed atmosphere of travelling that way.

The West Coast service was supplied by the Pacific Steam Navigation Company with two very passenger-like intermediate ships, which also covered the Carribean coast. For those who wished to disappear up the Amazon, Booth Line ran an intermediate service as far up as Manaus. Booth Line was always called 'Maggie Booths' amongst seamen; apparently a lady called Margaret took a good hand in boardroom affairs.

So there it was, a system running to time, stretching not only around South America, but all over the world, line by line.

The main lines which had ships carrying more than twelve passengers on their routes included Anchor, Peninsular and Oriental, New Zealand Shipping, Furness Withy, Elder Dempster, Canadian Pacific, Orient, Cunard, Shaw Savill, Ellermans, Union Castle and Blue Funnel. Cargo lines carrying twelve passengers were innumerable and covered almost anywhere that anyone could want to go. Twelve passengers was the Board of Trade limit before extra safety precautions were applied to a ship. Any vessel carrying over ninety-nine people aboard had to have a doctor.

It is often said that no British ship sailed with exactly one hundred souls; one over ninety-nine required a doctor, and he made the total one hundred and one.

All this sort of information didn't come from correspondence courses, it came from chatting, asking questions, but most important, listening. I'd only learned the ramifications of logging in Sweden because the Second Mate felt chatty one morning there. A great source of general information was to be gleaned at the informal gathering which occupied almost every evening, between tea and sundown on the main deck, outside the Chief Engineer's accommodation, near number four hatch. The Chief would step out for a breath of air, somebody would stop to chat, and so on. Anybody joined the group, but the younger you were the less you said, although questions were always welcomed.

This was the sort of thing that an apprenticeship was about. Different and varying jobs around the ship were a great thing, but also getting to know the type of people you would be working with and as much about other ships as possible to compare with your own.

In the tropics when the sun was setting in a clear sky, one diversion was for us to look for the Green Flash. You had to watch the sun disappearing for about its last three minutes; when it had gone from sight below the horizon you were meant to see a green flash. I often saw the sight, some always, and some never. So each evening there was a deathly hush for about four minutes, then odd cries of: 'Did you see it?' Jan was mystified by the whole performance and when it was over, he, ever helpful as usual, would add his contribution.

> 'Red sun at night
> We're all full of shite,'

and walk away thoughtfully.

I was told much later that it was not a natural phenomenon, but an optical illusion. The sun sets very quickly in the tropics and is usually very red; so if you have been concentrating on a red disc which suddenly vanishes to nothing, the eye gives the brain the dead opposite colour, which is green. I always felt sorry for the ones that never saw it; they probably did, but would not own to it in case one of the usual little leg-pulls was being perpetrated somehow.

Bridge work went on. Cleaning and polishing it, chipping and scraping it, learning little bits all the time: a chipping hammer must not be too sharp or the steel under the rust would get badly marked; scrapers scraped better when sharp. Wood scraping needed very sharp scrapers and Jan thoughtfully knocked off a file from Chippy for us to keep on the job. 'Yarp so yave mit,' he explained in his own deplorable langauge, of which I could decipher most by now; syntax was obviously something he thought had to do with a brothel.

One job was to make a check on all the ships' flags, which included two sets of International Code flags, that is A to Z and 0 to 9, all two yards in length. Amongst the locker of courtesy ensigns there was no Argentinean flag, which did not please the Third Mate, Mate or, very particularly, the Old Man. Some countries handed out heavy fines for vessels arriving without courtesy flags, and nobody was quite sure how strict the Argentine was. It was decided to fly 'J' flag, which was nearest to the Argentine one. The 'J' flag meant, 'I am going to send a message by semaphore,' but flown in the courtesy place it was hoped it would pass unnoticed. It did, but as soon as we got in, the agent's runner was sent hot-foot for the proper thing.

Another fact that emerged was that we had no spare house flag, and the one we had been using was filthy. The Mate told us to wash the old one, with the strictest instructions that it was to be washed carefully in cold water and Teepol. After the Mate had gone for his afternoon nap, the Old Man appeared with a packet of Daz, doled out some in a bucket with his instructions to add boiling water from the galley geyser. Obey the last order, as the old saying went. The thing came out uni-coloured and not very nice-coloured at that. The Mate did his nut when he came up at sixteen hundred. He was going to have us wash all the bloody code flags in our own time, and so on. Luckily the Old

Man, hearing the noise, came up and confessed it was his fault; this secretly pleased the Mate because it meant he'd have the edge on the Old Man for a day or two. I suggested that it might be painted, and was shouted down; it got painted and lasted well but nobody remembered that it was my idea.

The medical side of things, I found, was handled by the Chief Steward. However the Master, being responsible for everything in the end, naturally wanted to know if a patient's trouble was more than a quick plaster or a swift dose of 'Black Draught' would cope with. Black Draught you only had once because the mind told the body, if the body had not already realised, never ever to get constipated again. It tasted far worse than Hank had smelled.

So, once the Master was called in, a back-up team used to accumulate. The Second Officer was a must because he had taken the most recent Board of Trade certificate; this meant that he had had to produce a valid First Aid certificate with his entry papers. The Chief Officer joined in because he wanted the patient back on deck working. The Chief Engineer coupled on just in case it was one of his men, who were wanted back down below working. The Second Steward closed in on the group, on the excuse of serving coffee all round, to learn medical wisdom and, with no Hippocratic Oath involved, to spread the facts of any illness round the ship.

By this time the cabin was full, but often the Bo'sun and Chippy would turn up with a reason for seeing the Mate. They usually remained leaning against the door jambs with suitably long, but helpful-looking faces. Being on the outer edge, they could spread the word of anything interesting before the Second Steward.

You can never talk to a naval architect about the ship he is sitting in, but he will tell you oceans about others. So it was with the Old Man's back-up team. They would discuss every disease or illness they had come across on previous ships but the patient had to remain patient.

Treatment was usually temporarily decided upon when it was getting near the Second Mate's lunchtime; known as a seven-bell lunch because it took place at eleven-thirty. The back-up team would by this time have become a committee and further wrangling would be unfair with a lost member. The next move was to give the invalid a couple of aspirins, tell him to rest up and come back in the evening.

After lunch the Old Man would get out the Shipmasters' Medical Guide and have a read up. The Guide, coupled with a Board of Trade standard-stocked medicine chest, was a very comprehensive and clever work.

The Old Man, nearly or really having made up his mind after the reading, would then approach various members of the back-up team. Holding the book with a thumb somewhere in its pages his members came to sense; the cover was an ominous blood red. He would seek their opinions, which could vary from '. . . Well, that's what the Surgeon in my last ship said, Sir, just before he dropped dead,' to a more down-to-earth, 'Buggered if I know, Sir.' He was left with the can to carry as usual.

The evening came and the seaman would appear in front of the Old Man and the Chief Steward. Every ill person feels better in the evening, and an afternoon's reflective boredom, coupled with the rest, often ended up with that most sensible medical procedure; find out how the patient feels like treating himself and concur, observing closely with interest the result and hoping that he does not drop dead before he can be foisted onto the nearest hospital.

Years before my time it appears that the Shipmasters' Medical Guide was set up by members in conjunction with the Medical Chart. Treatment was a dose of twenty-three or a daily dose of number forty-one, and so on. The tale is told of the Master who said to the Chief Steward:

'Give this man a dose of number thirty-two.'

'But Sir, Sir, we have run out of thirty-two.'

'Then give him a double dose of sixteen.'

The one thing that was never allowed to happen was for anybody but the Master to see the Guide. Even a non-hypochondriac could develop at least eight consecutive diseases and internal troubles, together with a severe nervous condition, if left with the book overnight; it had happened so often before, apparently.

Nowadays nearly all Second Officers seem to be married to nurses and medical peril on the sea gets a bit more rational. Seriously, though, if you are really in a jam, there is a Rome Radio Medical Service you can phone on the R/T and have a specialist on the line in minutes.

The Medical Guide created for every eventuality for, on the last page, handily was printed "A Short Burial Service at Sea'. In fact, every little thing that could be thought of was. Passing the small cabin with an entrance to the deck, in case something contagious occurred, I found the Second Steward polishing in it. Remarking on general things, and getting satisfactory answers until it came to the bunk, I asked him why it was made up with such a big turn-down, and got the reply that it kept a patient's shoulders and upper body warm. I exclaimed that heat was not necessary in the hot weather; he then quietly told me that the real reason was that if the patient died there was plenty of sheet and blanket to draw over the head.

Smoking on the bridge was forbidden. As a result only the most hardened smokers would ever try smoking on the wheel and even then only for a couple of desperate drags before a quick extinguish was made; this was when the wheelmen were relieved every hour for ten minutes so they could have a smoke. Lighting a cigarette was possible for a wheelman, but getting rid of the exhaled smoke had its problems. One of the army dodgers quietly boasted that he smoked frequent and whole cigarettes while on the wheel; nobody expressed much belief.

On the Old Man's deck, which was the one directly below the bridge, there was also a very smart cabin named the Owner's Cabin, which was for some reason fitted with a voice pipe from the rear of the bridge. The Old Man, on inspection one Sunday, decided to take a look at the Owner's Cabin and found it full of layer upon layer of stale cigarette smoke. The army dodger had been quietly exhaling his smoke down the voice pipe for many days. The row that ensued was great, but luckily short-lived.

Officers were not meant to smoke during the four-hour period they were on watch. As a result, instead of the officer keeping a lookout ahead he kept a fair amount of his watch looking out over the after rail of the bridge for the Old Man, while taking a smoke.

Our Second Officer was smoking one afternoon when the Old Man had not taken his customary nap as expected, and arrived on the bridge. There was time to put the burning cigarette in his pocket hopefully. The Old Man took delight in chatting to him until being able to remark with relish, 'All right, Mister, you'd better go and put the fire out before it spreads too far.' The Second made a dive for the fire buckets as the Old Man disappeared. He stood there in his underpants examining a destroyed pocket, some lining and small hole in his trousers, when my mate decided to make the most leaden remark of his young career. He turned brightly to me and said,

'So that's why we have fire buckets up here, so the officers can put themselves out; I wonder if they use individual buckets or not.'

The Second's language was atrocious and we thought we'd better go and find a job elsewhere on the bridge.

The Third Mate told us that evening about an occurrence on another company ship, whose Master was well known as a right tartar. The Second was up taking a forenoon sight and had a cigarette tucked in his left hand fingers while manipulating his sextant. The Tartar suddenly arrived on the bridge and the Second in a moment of panic threw his sextant over the side. While, with a confused red face, he was stubbing out his cigarette, the Tartar remarked drily, 'So you see, Mister, how hazardous it can be to smoke on the bridge.' With sextants at about thirty pounds, it had been an expensive smoke. Curiously he did not get much sympathy from anybody; it was not the done thing for anyone to throw a lighted cigarette overboard, and that in effect was what he had done.

I'd taken up smoking myself. As a child and schoolboy I had never seen anything in the habit and could not understand anybody who did. Duty Free cigarettes were ten shillings for two hundred and dirt cheap, so at the age of seventeen I started; greed comes in many forms, but this was the most negative sort I ever took part in.

Suddenly it was Christmas Eve evening, and nothing happened. The next morning we got up at the usual time and my mate went to switch the deck lights out while I went to the bridge for orders as usual. The Mate greeted me with a 'Merry Christmas' and instructions to tidy the bridge up and take the rest of the day off. Bridges always get untidy overnight, teacup rings need wiping off, that signal halyard looks slacker than the rest, a slight shift of wind has blown some wood shavings out from somewhere and of course the brass needs cleaning.

I think that was really all the Mate was after. He wanted to see how fast the brass could be done when it was a 'job and finish', the crafty bastard; because for the rest of the voyage there were always rumblings from him about taking longer than had been taken on Christmas Day.

Breakfast was normal, except for the fact that two eggs were served instead of the customary one. The fact that there was no 'Something' was meant not to be noticed.

The morning was spent sitting around and chatting; the beer issue included an extra two bottles per person but not, of course, including apprentices.

Lunch was an affair of soup, fish, turkey and duff.

The near-traditional question from the Steward to the Old Man of did he want stuffing; the reply, with a very steely smile, was, 'Yes, I want stuffing and you may inform the whole pantry staff of the fact.'

The duff was superb and so was the sauce that went with it. Whistling is bad luck on board ships. The only exception and indeed requirement, was for the person who got the job of stoning any fruit that was to go into a duff or such. While the Chief Cook could hear his sidekick whistling, he knew that no fruit was being eaten.

The sauce was constructed on Christmas morning in the Chief Steward's cabin with the aid of Connie Onnie and two bottles of rum. Something else went into it, but nobody would quite remember what, as by no means all the rum made it.

After lunch the catering staff laid out a cold buffet and knocked off for the day.

The early afternoon was very quiet, but the odd people I saw were obviously a bit whistled. Later we were invited into one of the alleyway cabins for a drink. We protested and got the answer that it was Christmas Day. So we crept quietly down to a cabin filled with people going away good-oh with Las Palmas brandy that had been zealously saved, and not only for that cabin by the sounds nearby.

I started my glass, with kindly encouragement from the host, who could see I did not like it. 'If you can't get it down you, work it up you.' Then raised voices and a fight started nearby. I put my glass down, well unfinished, and made off to our cabin, where my mate joined me shortly after. We sat reading and thinking no more of the matter when a message came that the Mate wanted to see us on the bridge.

We got up there to find the Mate in a cold fury. We had been in accommodation that we had been told not to enter. Yes Sir. We had been drinking. Just a taste, Sir. We had been fighting. No Sir. We were to get off the bridge. Aye, aye Sir.

We sat mystified about the affair. It was certainly the first time that there was nothing of a twinkle in his eye, which there always had been before when he was swearing at us for something, albeit we might have to peer very hard.

The Third Mate dropped by before his watch and the mystery was partly cleared up. Apparently the fight had developed into a brawl, complete with cut eyebrows, bleeding noses and split lips, before it ended. In the patching-up-cum-enquiry it appeared that everybody had been adamant that we did not start the fight! Start it! We had only heard it start, just before evacuating.

It seems that our trouble had been caused by some big mouth going to the Old Man and telling him of the fight and adding: 'But the cadets did not start it!' The Old Man had hit the deckhead and stormed onto the bridge and bawled at the Mate: 'Your bloody apprentices have been in the middle of a drunken fight; you had better sort them out.' Oh dear me. How misunderstandings do start.

Boxing Day was not a holiday and the morning orders were an ominous: 'Carry on up here and be outside the Old Man's cabin at nine o'clock.' Before we reported to his cabin we agreed on a policy at least said soonest mended. As it happened we did not get the chance. The Mate marched us in to where the Old Man was sitting at his desk with his cap and our indentures before him; keelhauling at least.

'You did not lie to the Mate last evening,' as a statement, but one which required an answer.

'No, Sir.'

'Your shore leave is stopped for one week when we get to B A and if I find you drinking again I'll tear these indentures up. Now get out.'

Back at work twenty minutes later the Mate turned up and addressed us, 'And, when the Master has finished tearing your indentures up, I shall nail you to the awning spars for the passage home: by the balls.' The Mate was friends again.

So there it was. Christmas. There had been a serious fight by day, and by night the ship had steered a Las Palmas brandified course southwards. Nothing said to anybody else; only casualty – cadets' shore leave for a week. Unfair? Not really; we were different, we were apprentices, and two seventeen-year-olds maybe needed a tight rein: after all, the old bastard was more or less responsible for us, and this was one of the times he wished he was not.

What started the fight? Somebody taking drunken exception to something that did not concern him, except that he came from near Liverpool.

'What are the fifty-three articles that a Liverpool fireman takes to sea?'

'A pack of cards and a sweat rag.'

Over many Christmastimes spent at home and aboard ship, apart from the first boring and disastrous one, I still rather feel that Christmas aboard ship had a great advantage. It started on Christmas Eve evening; Christmas Day was Christmas Day;

Boxing Day was a working day. There was none of the long run-up that happens ashore.

The first landfall at the Plate was some low-lying Uruguay, and the vessel passed on to pick up a pilot for the passage along the buoyed channel to Buenos Aires. Our size of ship was not a problem. The large regular trading refrigerated liners run by Blue Star, Houlder Brothers and Royal Mail were built with twin screws to aid steering in shallow water when a ship was 'smelling the ground'. We were told that to go to ports further upriver twin screws were pretty vital. Anchoring about four miles off a beautiful-looking Buenos Aires we waited for about two hours before going in; it was a handy time to get mooring ropes on deck. Chippy crept round his precious hatch wedges loosening them.

Nearing the entrance to the New Port where we were to berth we made fast to two tugs, one for'd and one aft. We carried our own towing spring, which was a heavy wire with a thick coir pennant on the end. The tug threw us a light heaving line which one of the army dodgers made fast to the spring, which we then slacked away. We had just slacked away the coir pennant and were starting on the wire when there was a splash and a shout from the tug. The knot in the heaving line had come adrift, so we had six fathoms of heavy wet coir to heave in by hand, because the warping winch was not at its best. We started again with the heaving line made fast by an annoyed Jan.

When the tug was all fast, Jan cornered the army dodger for a discussion on knots.

'Most seamen use a bowline for that job; a few use a clove hitch which is only after all a jamming hitch with its arse kicked in. But you decide to tie a snowball hitch.'

'What's a snowball hitch?' asked the army dodger.

'It melts in the sun,' said Jan, turning away disgustedly.

I asked the Second later why we used our towing spring instead of the one visible on the tug. He explained that we could have done, but it would be added to the tug's bill as an extra.

We passed slowly through the docks and up to our berth. Sliding by some of the several British tramps, I witnessed another manifestation of the leg-pulling of Geordies, in which the rest of the Merchant Navy seemed to combine, chiefly because they can be rather a clannish river of people. To the calls by one of our A.B.s, 'Any Geordies aboard?' the reply could be, 'Aye, man, I'm Jarrow and there are two South Shielies. We'll be round after you've docked.' The next ship's answer to the question could be a flat, 'No, we're an all-white crew.' Another might hail us, and to our A.B.'s delighted reply of 'Yes,' would then shout across, 'Well, shoot the bastards.' No offence taken and none was meant; but still when I hear the cry over the water of 'Any Geordies aboard?' I cock my ear for the reply, which is often very original; and sometimes is thrown by a disguised Tyneside voice.

I found it rather strange to be tying up to the berth after five weeks at sea. Four ropes and a wire backspring made our end snug for a long stay. Galvanised circular rat guards were placed round the lines to stop rats joining or leaving that way as they are notorious disease carriers; the Black Death of the Middle Ages is attributed by many to rats and ships. We did not have rats as far as we knew, but there was always the chance that some had been picked up unknowingly. British ships were inspected for lack of rats while in the UK and a Deratization Certificate issued by Port Health authorities, which is eagerly sought after by other officials in places of call.

Having finished tying up and letting go the tugs, we started topping derricks and stripping two of the three tarpaulins from the hatches. Chippy bustled round collecting his cherished hatch wedges and hiding them under lock and key. It was of course the height of summer in B A, but as he said, once bitten twice shy, and he was not running the risk of the Argentino stevedores wanting them to light barbecues.

People from ashore came and went and we heard that we would not be starting cargo until the next morning. The Second Officer came round with a sub list, as everybody would want advances of pay in a port like this. The Second Steward came round with the mail. I had not heard from home for nine weeks, and it was distracting to have to continue working with my three letters burning a hole in my pocket. The last job was to get a pot of whitewash and a brush from Four Eyes as the Mate said he had something he wanted doing later.

After tea there was a long queue outside the Second Officer's cabin of people waiting to pick up their subs. I joined it and got the pound that I had put in for, surprised that it had been given with my shore leave stopped. Old Sparks was there and observed wryly, 'You see them all bright of mind and smartly dressed, but try being near the gangway when they start trickling back.'

When everybody who was going seemed to have left the ship, the Mate told me to get my whitewash, and paint about the bottom eight feet of the gangway. Explaining as I marked, 'It's no use putting rat guards on all the mooring lines and leaving a bloody great gangway for them to saunter up; but it so happens that rats don't like crossing anything white at night, particularly if it is illuminated by our gangway light, as it is going to be. It is not necessarily Argentine rats I want to stop, but rats that may have got off other ships and could have come from anywhere in the world with all sorts of possible diseases. In any case the crowd will get themselves into a horrible state after all this time with little or no beer, so the white will help them find the gangway when they get back.'

With nearly everybody ashore, the business of no shore leave began to bite. Hank was still aboard, reading several sheets of newspaper racing pages that had come in his mail. It was obvious that his sub would be spent on any local horse-racing that took place. I asked him if he used any system.

'Oh, certainly,' he said, his eyes lighting with interest. 'I tried several in my younger days, but for the last twenty years I've stuck to the same system. It's quite simple. I look carefully through the runners and pick the horse's name with the nearest connection to the sea. That is the one I back.'

'How does it work?' I asked.

Hank looked me in the eyes and said slowly, 'Since I have been doing the horses in this way, I must have lost hundreds of pounds!'

I moved on to chat to the Chief Engineer. He said that Buenos Aires had always been a port that seaman looked forward to visiting, but the Police or Vigilantes would pick up any seaman that caused any sort of trouble instantly. He said that, when he had visited the port years before, the Vigilantes had their own way of dealing with jailed miscreants the next morning. They did not bother with magistrates or fines. All hands were turned to sweeping streets, cleaning statues, and other jobs which kept the place smart. I asked him if he had every been caught out in that way.

'Of course not, you cheeky little bugger, what sort of person do you think I am?' he snarled.

'I'm sorry, Chief,' I apologised.

The Chief mellowed and said reflectively, 'I used to take a pair of cotton working gloves ashore with me, just in case, you know!'

We were just going off to sleep that night when there were loud voices and sounds of the gangway being abused. On going out to look, we found Jan being half carried up it by the ship's nightwatchman and the Old Man. Apparently Jan had tried to crawl up the gangway, but had slipped under the manropes and disappeared into the gangway net. The Old Man, who had been having a last smoke, had come to give the watchman a hand. They all got to the top of the gangway where Jan straightened up, smiled at the Old Man and mumbled:

'Yngemnscolnuinjdgers.'

The Old Man said goodnight and left, just as Jan collapsed onto the steel deck.

We carried Jan aft, put him in his bunk and loosened his clothing; all three of us shaking with laughter which made the job about twice as hard. It was lucky that the Old Man did not understand Jan's language as it would have been embarrassing for all. Jan had given him the highest accolade he knew: 'You are a gentleman and a scholar and a fine judge of arse!'

The night was gently rent at intervals by the sounds of returning crew members; all having had a fair time.

Next morning five gangs of stevedores arrived and commenced discharging using ship's derricks. It was a bit of a rush to start with: five different gangs all wanting the derricks at their hatch topped or lowered a bit and expecting instant action. In several cases their will had just been done when a more senior chap turned up and wanted them rigged just a bit different; breakfast was late by the time everybody was happy.

The state of most of the crew had to be seen to be believed. Nine weeks without a run ashore meant that far more beer had been drunk than was strictly necessary; walking and talking were alright, but anything else was difficult. As Deaf Charlie put it, 'It's like a Portuguese wedding, everybody talking and nobody listening.' Jan was surprisingly well and explained that the secret of early morning health was to get a lot inside you early and then come back and get plenty of sleep. I did not like to ask if he always started his sleep from the top of the gangway onwards.

The first day in port meant a lot of small and varying jobs not needing much concentration, so no real work was lost by the carousal of the previous night. Subsequent shore-going settled into evening jaunts rather than wild nights.

New Year occurred and nobody really took much notice except for the very few Scots aboard, who by this time had been able to smuggle some of their native spirit aboard so they could do the honours properly. They took a down-to-earth attitude, and the chief part of the ritual was to throw the cork of each newly opened bottle firmly overboard.

I had stayed up to see what happened at midnight and I was glad that I did. At twelve, every ship in the port started blowing their whistles, not continuously, and not to any set pattern, just long or short blasts intermittently for about ten minutes. The boom of passenger ships' whistles, the roars from the tramps, the raucous yells from a couple of motor ships with air whistles, all at varying distances, was a very impressive sound. One or two were late starters and they seemed to have more water in their whistle lines than the others and sounded like frightened pigs farting until the steam got through. No matter, it made the noise all the more variable. I've never missed the opportunity of listening since; Auld Lang Syne can always come later, after the joyous cacophony of ships going slightly mad is over. Forecastle bells were also rung. By tradition eight bells from the oldest man in the ship to mark the Old Year's passing were rung, and then another eight from the youngest of the crew to mark the coming of the New. This was the only time that sixteen bells were rung furiously so that their different tones added to the uproar. The peace and quiet that returned when everybody had finished was very noticeable, definitely a case of the night being unshattered! Leaning over the rail one afternoon smokoe, we watched the Ship Chandler's wagon turn up with fresh provisions. Our dry stores had been stocked well up before leaving the UK and, used carefully with fresh, would last for months.

Deaf Charlie recalled being on a Greek tramp ship many years before in a small Mexican port, when their stores turned up in a bullock-drawn cart. The two men helped load the stores, they slaughtered the ox for fresh meat, chopped up the cart for galley firewood and then signed on the ship as A.B.s. A good study in logistics, I thought.

Smokoe over, the A.B.s returned to their own work with Four Eyes, and we were told off to help load the stores. Cadets were handy in this way: we were put onto an all-day job and then taken off for any odd jobs that came up. The deck crowd seemingly preferred one job that they could get on with, and show some result at the end of the day; being pulled off and on jobs did not suit them at all.

Two cadets came to visit from the British tramp ahead of us. They had come from New York and their next stage was to Australia. This was a thing. Liners went from A to B and back to A again. Tramps could go from A to B to C to D and so on for the full two years the Articles lasted, and for longer, providing the vessel was then loading and discharging in the direction of the UK. We had had no inkling of what our next charter would be.

Our next move was to ask the Mate if we could visit the ship ahead, explaining to him that it was not really shore leave to do so.

'Very well,' he said, 'but be careful what you do over there. Remember, this is the seventh and last day of your leave stoppage.'

She was not that different from our ship, being an ex-wartime Fort boat. The cadets lived in amongst the deck officers' accommodation, but with a much smaller cabin than ours. Their one big advantage was that they could get beer aboard, which, when they heard we'd been dry for ten weeks, they offered freely. Their Second Mate turned up and accepted a beer as the conversation got general. Their two cadets were bemoaning the fact that they had to start painting the white line round the vessel's black hull the next morning, and went on to say what they thought about shipping companies that used this style as part of the livery of their ships. Their Second chipped in to explain why it was there.

'In the days of sail, every ship that went to Far Eastern waters was armed, and usually painted with a broad white band forrard to aft at the level of her gun ports. Even when the ships ceased to carry armament, the white stripe was still carried, as all the pirates and bad hats had got used to the idea that it meant a well-defended ship. You see many ships going around with a white line, albeit now only about ten inches wide, but if you check on their company's history, you'll nearly always find early connections with Far Eastern trade.'

I mentioned the two debâcles when Las Palmas brandy had got loose, and that in my opinion it was a funny way to have a watch system, darkness or no darkness.

Their Second shrugged his shoulders. 'These things happen. We don't like it, but the biggest of all things in this game is that the job keeps going. You'll find yourself as officer of the watch and left on the wheel one night, but you'll be surprised who creeps up to the bridge and gives you a spell; people you never knew could even steer! It's a nuisance when it happens, but it's infrequent enough to be funny afterwards. I remember one Christmas when we were miles from anywhere; I knew two of my watch had faded out of the picture, but I still had a wheelman. Suddenly, from the wheelhouse door, I heard through the darkness, "Sec., will you take the wheel for a bit while I slip down for a slash?" I said yes, and moved from the bridge wing in time to have the unscrewed wheel thrust into my hands as the bastard disappeared down the ladder. So before I could take over the steering I had to refit the wheel, all in darkness.

'I'd been steering and cursing for about half an hour when our old Chief Engineer slid into the wheelhouse, said he'd heard I had some trouble with the steering and that I'd better let him try things for a bit. The old Chief did over an hour until the new watch was due to arrive; just his way of helping to keep the job going.'

Their Second Steward stuck his head through the door, with tactful suggestion that their Old Man had a guest.

The talk went on of people and ships; it seemed that the bigger the accident or disaster the funnier it was; assuming there had been time for hindsight and that nobody had been killed. Then came the sound of two sets of footsteps coming down their Old Man's ladder; he was obviously seeing his guest off. The footsteps stopped outside the cabin, there was a knock and the curtain was pulled back.

'Well, there are the lads, enjoying themselves,' said our Old Man to the stranger who was his host. They walked on down the alleyway leaving the pair of us thunderstruck and the rest of the cabin killing itself with mirth.

That bloody Mate of ours had let us walk straight into it, knowing our Old Man was visiting. We had another beer and went back to our own ship.

At nine o'clock the next morning we were up before the Old Man. There was no cap on his desk and no indentures; maybe he had torn them all up in fury.

'You were drinking on that ship,' he stated firmly, but not with the venom he had used previously. 'I suppose you are going to tell me that you got over there, and then did not like to refuse the hospitality out of politeness.'

I could not keep a straight face but then, controlling it, I answered as politely as possible, 'As a matter of fact, Sir, we had thought of suggesting something like that, but were not sure if it would be acceptable or not.'

'Well it bloody well isn't. Shore leave stopped for seven days. You two seem to think the Chief Officer and I were never cadets ourselves. Get out!'

As we turned to, my mate remarked in a kindly voice, 'I think that our dear old dad is mellowing towards us. He has not forbidden us to visit other ships; when we put in for our weekly sub of a pound it seems to get paid out OK. I suspect he just doesn't want us to go up town.'

'He seems to regard us as potential troublemakers, but what trouble can we cause against this town's three million population? In any case, didn't you get friendly advice and warnings from your people about how to behave?'

My mate looked thoughtful. 'Yes, from my father, which for him was remarkably intelligent: never do anything that you would be ashamed to tell one, or the other, of your parents about. That, after reflection, I took to mean: have a fair time, but don't blab the wrong thing to your mother. Did you get handy hints for first-trip apprentices?'

'Not from home as such, I think they'd rather given up. There was one old boy in my village, who has knocked around the world for most of his life; he gave me a reasonable field of action. He held my elbow firmly and, looking into my eyes with his grey rheumy ones, pronounced earnestly, "Try anything once, except incest, or Morris dancing."'

Chipping and scraping went on, but mostly scraping because the noise of a banging hammer could distract the stevedores and maybe cause an accident. The ship was hot now, with little or no wind to ventilate generally. Cold water for drinking was out; the store-room fridges would chill two buckets of water a day and the Chief Engineer did not really like to be asked to give permission for these. The chilled water came to one good glassful per man each day.

We had noticed that our Arab firemen had produced some small canvas bags. The top was sewn up except for a pipe at each corner, one longer than the other. These were filled with water and hung out on deck in the shade of an awning. My dear old schoolmaster had been telling me for years that Evaporation Causes Cooling, without much belief on my part at all. However, once the water soaked through the canvas, science did its stuff and a beautifully cool drink emerged when the bag was tipped; the shorter pipe letting the water out and the longer one letting the air in.

I wanted one. The Arab firemen would always offer a cool drink from their chatis, but it was obviously a bit off to use somebody else's. The answer was to make my own, but where to get the gear was another matter. Four Eyes had it no doubt, and what Four Eyes had, Four Eyes kept. Guile and cunning were needed. I hoped it was a case of 'Softlee, Softlee, Catchee Monkey' to borrow a West African phrase.

I waited until the Chief and Second Engineers were talking together and asked the Second for a boiler gauge glass, telling him what I wanted it for. I then went to Chippy and asked him how difficult it was to break the glass into two uneven lengths. It appeared that this was a very difficult job, but he would see what he could do. He was back after work that day with the job done perfectly, of course.

I had cut the legs off a pair of dungarees to convert them to shorts, and kept the cut-off legs; I never threw anything away on that trip! I borrowed a palm, needle and sail-twine from one of the A.B.s, then sat outside and started sewing my chati.

Chippy had told Four Eyes. The Chief and Second had told

others. I sewed slowly, very slowly, away until the entire ship's crew except Four Eyes had passed by and told me I was wasting my time doing the job in anything but canvas. I kept sewing slowly until everybody had had the chance to tell me at least five times each that canvas was the only way.

I had used a palm and needle before going to sea. There was plenty of time to make the stitching and the sewing in of the glass tubes a very neat job. Just before completion, I left the effort unattended where Four Eyes could inspect it.

The day came for the great test, and it was a complete and utter failure! Water poured from it faster than I could fill it, and nearly all the crew told me I should have used canvas.

That evening, shortly after tea, there was a bang on the door, and Four Eyes dumped a small piece of canvas on the table. He explained that if I wanted to make a chati I should use canvas. I thanked him profusely. I had been banking on the fact that once he saw I could use a palm and needle fairly well for a seventeen-year old, and having witnessed complete failure, he might just get his bloody mustard spoon out and cut me a small length of canvas.

Through the evening a procession of people turned up with small lengths of canvas, and explained that it was the proper gear for the job.

The Second Engineer turned up.

The Third Engineer turned up with some canvas that the Second still thought he had left.

Chippy turned up with some.

Jan turned up with some that Four Eyes still thought he had left.

After each visit the canvas was quickly stowed out of sight.

Hank turned up with some that Chippy still thought he had left.

One of the Arab donkeymen turned up, and after explaining in Arabic that canvas was best for the job, handed over some that the Second still thought he had left.

Deaf Charlie turned up with some that Hank still thought he had left, having pinched double the amount from Chippy in the first place.

The Chief Steward turned up with a piece that everybody still thought they had left; but Chief Stewards don't get to their position without craft.

The Mate turned up with what was apparently the very last piece of Fort Knox.

By now we seemed to have enough canvas to outfit a brigantine, if not a fully rigged sailing ship, with sails.

By chati-sewing hard, I had one operating a day or so later, but I had to remember to thank, or rethank, everybody individually. I am quite certain that cooled water is better for one than iced water, and in later years when iced water dispensers became common, I had as much guts trouble as everybody else who poured the stuff down onto an empty stomach.

Several of the crowd had taken to playing football on the wide grass border between the head of the dock and the fence surrounding the harbour area. There was an adjacent dock gate and guard house with a solitary small bar just outside. We took up football; one of us had to come back for flags and lights and then had no excuse to go ashore again as it was dark. It was pretty bloody obvious where the other one had gone!

We had never been stopped from going to the ship ahead, so the scheme was for the one of us to slide out to the bar and have a couple of beers, then on return the other would go ship visiting 'to change this bundle of magazines, sir.' Poor bundle of magazines, it was nearly worn away by the time we left, and it began to smell of beer.

So the beer problem was solved, but I wanted a look up town. Changing into my best dungarees and clean shirt, but still going ashore with the kick-about bunch, I kept going out of the dock gate, past the bar and away.

What a beautiful city BA was, with so many broad roads and open spaces. The only trouble with it was that you could enter nowhere decent without a tie and jacket; this included cinemas. Still, it was very pleasant to have a look around.

My mate or I used to creep off on alternate nights. The weekly pound went a fair way; beer was cheap and if one felt peckish on the way back to the ship there were cheap cafes where steak and chips cost just over a shilling.

There were two seamen's missions in BA. The British Sailors' Society ran one and the Catholics ran another, known as the Flying Angel. Very worthwhile places to visit, they would provide relative peace and quiet unless there was a do on. Any help, advice or information they would provide on the spot; if a ship wanted to arrange a football match, a picnic, or an outing of some sort, things were easily organized. Each mission was run by a padre and he had many willing female assistants of all ages who were very pleasant and hospitable.

The fourteenth night of shore leave stoppage passed. At nine o'clock in the morning the Old Man sent for us.

'You two have been sliding ashore while your leave is stopped.'

'Yes, Sir,' we said.

He enquired where we had been going, and we said to the missions.

'I'll bet it's the Catholic one mostly, they sell beer and the other one doesn't. You have deliberately defied my orders. I want your word that you will not go outside the dock gate again.' We gave it: no choice. I was a bit disgusted with the whole performance and spent most of my spare time on the ship ahead with a very alcoholic result.

I met the Old Man years afterwards in a public house in Sheffield, where he lived, purely by chance. We got chatting and he explained the tight rein he had kept us on. He did not like the idea of having two first-trip seventeen-year-olds with him. There should have been a more senior cadet. Years previously he had been in a ship with the same set-up and the two youngsters had run wild in every direction, ending up with one of them being killed and the other badly injured. He reiterated that as indentured apprentices we became under his guardianship; he was responsible to our parents. He said he would rather lose the entire crew overboard, as long as he could get the apprentices into port safely; otherwise it caused too much paperwork. I said I thought he should have explained at the time, instead of keeping men virtually in jail for four or five weeks. We went on to yarn about light subjects. He told me how he happened to hear that there was an apprentice who turned up at the mission in open-necked shirt and dungarees, unusual in itself. Then he heard that this gadget had a faintly unpleasant aroma, and that had given the game away. I had never quite been able to get rid of the smell of the cats' spew muck!

Discharging was going steadily; a few more days would see it complete. Once the 'tween decks were clear we started cleaning them, sometimes helped by one or two of the deck crowd. It was amazing how much rubbish accumulated even with such a clean cargo as woodpulp. Dunnage, that is the loose wood planks used to stow cargo on, had to be stacked, though we did not have very much of it.

It is frightening when one sees an accident about to happen and can do nothing about it: that split second seems to last for minutes. In the 'tween deck there were small trimming hatches at intervals; about three feet square with a hinged wooden lid to allow trimmers to get into the wings of the lower hold to trim certain types of cargo.

Chippy's unfavourite army dodger was working on the other side of the 'tween deck; an exasperated Four Eyes had found a way to get shot of him for a day or two. I was looking across the 'tween deck when I saw him just about to step on top of a trimming hatch which I could see had been left open for some reason. He disappeared through it. Fortunately, Chippy said unfortunately, he was carrying a piece of dunnage under each arm and these went into his armpits to stop him crashing into the near empty lower hold. It was comical to see him dangling with his head and shoulders above 'tween deck level and his legs thrashing about in the thin air of the hold. It was with barely suppressed mirth that we staggered round to lift him out; he could not move because both arms were jammed under the hatchway. We lifted him out and the only damage seemed to be deep grazing in the vicinity of his armpits. He was sent off to the Chief Steward with an escort, for patching. Chippy ostentatiously inspected the two bits of dunnage and proclaimed that there seemed to be no damage to them!

When it was all over, I said to Chippy, 'I don't see how a chap can fall like that and not dislocate his shoulders, or break an arm as they brought him up; at least you'd expect a broken collar bone.'

Chippy gave me his simple explanation: 'Because he's too bloody stupid!'

The Chief Officer was talking about trimming hatches and then about the subject of trimming in general later that evening, while we were standing on deck.

'And while on the subject of trimming, remember that when

you become officers, you will have to inspect trimming gangs' work; this will include disappearing down the odd trimming hatch, or more likely crawling into the darkness under hatch coverings with a torch. You must never ever go on that job without having a member of the ship's crew with you. He stands clear and sees you go in and makes absolutely certain that you come out! Trimming gangs are very often not the normal stevedores, or even professional trimmers; they can be casual riff-raff from just outside the dock gate. If you are going to cause them too much work you can find yourself shovelled in, but they dare not do it if you have somebody watching you. If you do get shovelled in and don't come out, everybody shrugs their shoulders and says what a terrible accident, knowing full well deliberation was involved; nothing could ever be proved.'

Chippy was of the same mind when it came to cement washing one of the two fresh-water tanks situated in the 'tween decks. These were the drinking water tanks which had to be cleaned, by Board of Trade regulation again, every six months; now cargo was clear of them, it was time to operate. In coating the interior of a tank, the tools used were a whitewash brush and a bucket of cement wash. The idea was to cover the inside and seemingly yourself in wet cement; I was starting to get a bit crafty, and wore a sou'wester. On one emergence from the tank, I was met by a steely-eyed Chief Officer, who looked me up and down, then remarked, 'I hope you have enough cement left to do at least some of the tank.' Saucy bastard.

Actually he was not far short of the mark, as usual. I thought my mate had flicked a bit of cement at me, so I just flicked a very little back; within seconds there was a flailing cement war. It was very enjoyable and I recommend it. Chippy, from outside the tank, showed the quick-wittedness which makes British Merchant Service Petty Officers the finest in the world. He stopped the battle in the only conceivable way, by shouting, 'Smokoe, lads.'

The tank was entered by an elliptical-shaped lid bolted low down in its side. Chippy stressed that we must never, ever, enter a tank without somebody standing outside who would know of the occupation. Otherwise he warned there was always the chance that some idiot would come and put the lid on.

'However,' he said, 'in this sort of small tank you can cheat on that score. The lid is oval, so take it and the securing nuts inside with you. Don't bring them out until you are just finished!'

The Chief Officer, as so often, had a bit to add, 'When you're a Third Mate you will be sent to inspect freshly-cemented double-bottom tanks. The foreman will stand outside the tank while you crawl through the interior to check each bay. You come out and you usually tell him it's OK. He says "Thanks" and signs to a boiler maker to put the lid on. You think you have inspected the finished work; as far as he is concerned you have just been checking round to see that all his men are out before the tank is closed.'

Now that the 'tween decks were clear, another job with Chippy turned up; one of the accommodation toilets had blocked up and two more on the same line were rather sluggish. The plumbing ran under the main deck, which was the same thing as the 'tween deck deckhead, so we could get at it by short ladders and precariously balanced boxes. Rods and canes and spanners were fetched from forward and we were ready to go.

'Now,' said Chippy, 'on this job we are trying to get the muck out at our end while we are at our end. Messy. Decide between you which is going to get covered in it, then that one can make up his mind to it and we will get on with the proceedings.' I lost, and climbed the ladder to start at the plugs while the other two backed up with spanners and so forth. On that sort of job things differ from ashore; you cannot dodge. I was of course helped by my mate calling up, 'Do you want me to go and find out what everybody has been eating?' and such like. My language in return consisted of well-known and well-worn single and double words, indelicate phrases of the sea. It took all day and I felt that any food or drink taken would have been unhygienic, so I fasted.

The Chief Officer, as usual, had words to say later. 'You smell a bit better now, but I was pleased to see that Chippy ran the exercise properly. So often you see three or four men all getting fairly dirty and playing around meanwhile, that's wrong, it needs one determined and keen volunteer. I take it that you were both keen and a volunteer?'

'I was very determined too, Sir,' I risked.

'Good. Well just hope you never get the same employment in a passenger ship; it is amazing the things that get into the system. Many seamen regard passengers as cattle, and the odd one or two sometimes suggest that they think cattle are a bloody sight cleaner, certainly in their sanitary arrangements.

'I remember when I had taken part in the removal of a particularly difficult and obscene article from the piping. That evening was a gala dinner with a dance afterwards; the settings were superb. It was all mess kits, dinner jackets and the occasional claw-hammer jacket, on the male side. The ladies were long-dressed and bejewelled, and a few with tiaras which were not out of place that evening. The ladies' scent coupled with perfect music made it a memorable occasion. It was entirely spoilt for me, because each time I looked over the happy and glittering throng I kept wondering, "Which of you dirty bastards put THAT down the crapper?"'

We were sitting at lunch the next day when the Old Man, coming back from the Agents later than usual, stuck his head round the saloon door and called to the Mate, 'Chief, we're fixed with grain; UK/Continent.'

This was the news we had been waiting for, and lunch ended quickly, everybody sensing that, with the Old Man going up to his cabin and ordering sandwiches, he would be calling for odd bits of information on various matters as he studied the Charter Party we had been fixed with. Chippy, having heard the news, was waiting for the Mate to come out of the saloon.

'Take the Gadgets with you and check the shifting board gear, just in case,' the Mate threw over his shoulder as he made a dive for his cabin mumbling about the Grain Regulations.

When we started with Chippy, I asked: 'Did the Mate mean check just in case there is any missing?'

'No,' grunted Chippy, 'he means just in case there is any left!'

Grain as a cargo was very liable to shift when the ship rolled, Chippy explained. Spare portable steelwork was provided with each new ship, that could be erected down the centre line of each hatch. At the top of these steel girders, boards were fitted vertically which would stop the grain shifting.

'We'll have a look through the 'tween decks just to make sure there is not any gear; I know there is none in the lower hold. It's unlikely there is any at all because I checked with Ali, the fireman, who's been on the ship for years, and he tells me that she carried a cargo of scrap iron about four years back, and that usually buggers things. They discharge the scrap, and the shifting board steelwork they take as a bonus. Some Mates try painting the shifting gear in a bright colour for identification. It doesn't work. It just warns the dockers to hide them carefully from any prying eyes of officers that might notice their loss and come looking.'

We did not find any sign and Chippy reported to the Mate a definite negative. The Mate was unperturbed as he had heard that our cargo would consist of a fair amount of bagged grain with the bulk. Bagged grain, loaded strategically, fitted the requirements of the Grain Regulations, which were promulgated by the Board of Trade. Everybody seemed to half-sneer about the Board and its works, but as far as I could see, we would have been in a funny way without them in many directions.

The rough scheme worked out was that we would load bulk in the lower holds; at the top the grain would be trimmed into the wings leaving a dish-like space in the hatch square which would be filled with bags. The 'tween decks would have bags in their wings and their square filled with bulk. The Mate and Second Mate kept talking about certain percentages of type of cargo in type of place, which would comply with the Grain Regulations. We still had not finished discharging by a long way, so they had daily huddles until their stratagem was complete. Their next step was to take the scheme up to the Old Man and ask him to find fault with it. This meant that the Old Man ran through their ideas and reckoning, asking as many awkward questions as possible. They were all pleased when no fault could be found; they had a double-checked loading plan for anybody to see.

The UK/Continent destination sounded fine, but one big snag was found. A copy of the Articles of Agreement had by law to be placed on show in the crew accommodation. The Continent, in Board of Trade parlance, meant a port between Brest and the Elbe river, by the way. The Articles had a clause in them about when the voyage ceased; specifically mentioned in ours was that the end of the voyage would be in the last port UK/Continent, and that would mean the ship paid off the crew for leave. The snag was that the Continent was crossed out and initialled by the Shipping Master who had signed us on. This would have been done at the Master's request and done before anybody had to sign the Articles. It was normal, legal, and a bloody nuisance. So it was a UK pay off only, if we went to the Continent the ship could sail outward without Articles ending.

There was talk of moving from BA to one or two of the smaller

Argentinean ports, but we eventually ended up loading the full cargo with only a shift of berth. As each hold finished, serious hatch cleaning started, Four Eyes and his deck crowd doing the mundane stuff, while the timber boards covering the bilges each side of the hold and the bilges themselves were reserved for Chippy and we apprentices. The bilges were about four feet deep, like two troughs running the length of each hold, interspersed by the ship's farming arrangement about every three feet, which turned the bilge into a series of bays. I could get in myself, or I could get bucket, dustpan and brush in comfortably, but all four together was rather a squeeze. Manipulating all four together was an extreme feat of agility and contortion. The content was as nauseating as it was interesting; the bilges had not been properly cleaned when somebody had said they had, obviously. Traces of iron ore mixed with grain and water plus, as my mate put it, 'several excellent specimens to be noted for our International Collection Record.' Apart from anything else, grain and water left together slopping about gave off a very funny odour. Chippy, in passing, warned us never to go into any badly ventilated space containing the same mixture; open bilges were safe enough he said. The bilges were coated with a bitumastic grease which was designed to withstand all reasonable bilge muck, and also to dry so it would not run in hot climates. It was not designed to withstand the heat of hot climates and the warmth of human bodies; it transferred its adherence to you very gently and very firmly. The colour was a rather pleasant purply mauve. So, after a few dummy runs, we found that it was just possible, if we moved quickly enough, to clean a bay before any grease started to transfer. The Chief Officer, as usual, was solicitous and, after enquiring if there was still any grease left in his bilges, suddenly asked:

'What's a tank side bracket? No? What's a margin plate? No?

Well, you've been cursing them for the last three days. How rude of you not even to know their names. This evening get your books out and draw a bilge section, labelling the parts. Nothing elaborate, just a rough sketch, and let me have it as soon as you finish.'

He was always like that. We used to get into some corners and covered in various things, but he certainly taught us ship construction. Of course, he couldn't resist asking for a sketch of the fresh-water tank from the inside, and it was not until I sat down and tried to start that I realised it was impossible. He settled smiling, for a plan view.

I did get him once, later. I was painting a section of bulwark, that is the solid ship's rail, when along he comes on his little afternoon inspection before taking over his watch. 'Sketch me a section of sheerstrake and bulwarks meeting and let . . .' I did not let him get further, as my hand flashed to my pocket for the rough drawing I had knocked up in the lunch-hour on chance. He just thanked me, without smiling, a certain sign that he was amused.

Late one afternoon my mate turned green. He was quite impressive. He had been in one of the holds and one of the sailors cleaning box-beams had waited until my mate was directly underneath before raking out a whole bay full of sulphur from a past cargo. I would not have thought sulphur was a thing to play games with, but the result was spectacular.

Chatting that evening, I suggested that we kept a list of the various things we had been covered in, rather like a bird-watcher's list.

'It's a good idea,' he ruminated, 'but impracticable. We've been in this game for about three months and think of the number already. If we have three years and nine months to go, I don't think we could find a big enough piece of paper, even if we wrote on a bog roll with a mapping pen. If ever I write my memoirs I'm sure it will be the dirtiest book ever written.'

The occupation called for short hair and short fingernails; easier to clean of course. I had been slightly apprehensive when early in the voyage I had asked the Chief Steward why cadets were issued with an extra bar of soap each week.

'You'll find out,' he had grunted.

Self cleaning with hot shower and soap was alright for surface work sometimes. The end of the day meant a small wad of cotton waste in the paraffin that Four Eyes used to soak his paintbrushes. Nailbrushes were handy but they wore out on the way home. My mate remarked that he hoped his dear old grey-headed mother never found out that her loved and previously cherished son had been reduced to cleaning himself with wire wool.

I should explain that the ship's bond, or shop, only sold cigarettes, tobacco and matches; so the scheme was to take enough soap powder and toothpaste to last a voyage. You do this on your second trip.

The smell of my dungarees still rankled. I could not get rid of it anyhow; I'd even tried changing the odour with only very temporary success. I was amused in later years when it was the 'in' thing with youngsters to fade and stain their jeans; all very amateur. I felt that they should have been able to lend them to a tramp-ship apprentice to wear just after the War, and have the job done by professionals; forty-eight-hour service!

A passing Jan suggested fug was the answer, but with his dialect he could have meant 'fog' or 'fig'. I sought out the Chief Steward and the Chief Engineer who both looked puzzled and denied any knowledge of the stuff. Late in the evening, sitting on the hatch with my mate, Hank and Deaf Charlie, Jan came past.

'Hey Jan,' called Hank, 'what is this Fug business?'

Jan was happy with sufficient audience to elucidate.

'Dey always tell me when I am young seaman: if Persil won't

do it, if Tide won't do it, if Daz won't do it, then Fug it!' Jan's cackle was nearly drowned by our roar of indelicate derision.

Discharge ended and we had to move to another berth in the docks for our grain. It was almost strange to get the order, 'Stand by, fore and aft,' usually shortened to just 'Fore and Aft,' after all this time; the forrard gang and the after gang separated to go their ways. In some posh ships the order was simply 'Stations,' which I always felt was rather silly. They must run around calling 'Stations' without ever saying if they meant Bus Stations, or Fire Stations, or even Railway Stations; no, one was just left to guess that it was Stations for entering or leaving harbour. The Royal Navy, according to Deaf Charlie, did the job almost over-properly by making the pipe, or announcement, over loudspeakers: 'Hands to Stations for entering Harbour. Clear lower deck,' with anything else added as necessary. There had apparently been quite a row before the war in the cruiser returning with Queen Maud's coffin from Norway. On the approach the pipe was made: 'Hands to Stations for entering harbour. Clear Lower Deck.' Pause. 'Stand fast Queen Maud!'

Starting to load the grain was impressive; instant small mountains. The small mountains did not seem to grow very much unless I did not look for a couple of days. It was back to routine ship maintenance and, apart from a lot of dust, not much seemed to happen.

The first occupation in the new berth had been to go with the Third Mate and sound around the outside of the vessel with the hand lead-line. The Third explained that we would be loading to a deep draught and our wily Chief Officer wanted to check for certain that there was enough water under the keel to do so. He had once been a junior officer in a ship which had completely loaded and then found herself unable to get off her berth because she was buried in the mud; red faces all round and some vacancies at the end of the voyage!

Our soundings round showed that there was plenty of water for all our purposes. Then the Old Man showed that he could be a bit wily too.

'Hang that line overside and let it all soak for a little while; ask the Mate if I can borrow you two and his tape-measure for a few minutes,' he called down from his deck.

The Mate's tape-measure was a large leather-cased one. It was reckoned to be about the most important piece of gear in the ship; you could tell this by the fact that everybody who borrowed it returned it promptly after use, instead of trying to hang on to it, as with any other tools or equipment.

We carried the wet line up to the boat deck and started to check the measurements between marks. The Old Man was quite delighted when he found one of the marks was a foot out of place.

'Don't ask me how,' he said, shaking his head, 'but this sort of thing seems to happen. If you have the sounding-line out, it's wet, and you have a few minutes, check it: as you can see, it can pay. Now let's see what you know about the way the line is marked.'

This last was inevitable. It was one of the many things that people liked asking cadets, including BoT examiners at ticket time. However, unusually for him, the Old Man had slipped up. As he questioned, behind him on the deck was the line flaked out to dry. A twenty-fathom crib in full view.

The hand lead-line was marked to twenty fathoms and then had another ten fathoms spare for the height of the ship's side. The twenty separate fathoms were not all marked, and the unmarked fathoms were known as deeps.

The marks were constructed of leather, white linen, red bunting and blue serge. The colour would show them during daylight and the four different textures could be felt at night; in the dark and the cold with freezing hands the wisest way was to check with your tongue.

On returning the Mate's tape-measure, he enquired if everything was in order. I told him of the mark being out of place.

'Huh,' he grunted. 'It shows the need in this game to check everything as often as possible; even if some idiot hasn't shifted something, things seem to shift themselves. The mythical "Man from Liverpool" often gets the blame.

'Yes,' he ruminated, 'but lead-lines caused me a lot of bother when I was serving my time.'

This was quite good; I should have been working, but if the Mate wanted to talk about his apprenticeship it was fine with me.

'There were four of us in the ship; the officers and crowd were fine and the Old Man was as good as gold. We turned round on the continent without paying off and for the next trip the Old Man's wife turned up. She soon showed her colours as a bloody trouble-making old bastard; you name it and she complained or found fault over it. We four nicknamed her Mark Ten and kept out of her way as much as possible. Well, as is usual aboard ship, she did not take long to find out that she had a nickname. She was even heard boasting quietly to the Agent's wife in one port that her husband's boys had given her the secret name of Mark Ten. We headed for home and somehow she found out the derivation of her nickname. She gave the four of us absolute hell, demanded that her husband give us rotten reports, almost spat at any of us she saw and generally gave the impression that she thought we should be jailed on arrival.'

I had not seen the point, and the Mate asked, 'What is mark ten on a lead line?'

'A piece of leather with a hole in it,' I answered, and then laughed.

'Well there you are; always be careful if you give anybody a nickname. Now bugger off and do some work.'

The actual lead on a lead-line weighed seven pounds and had a recess in the bottom. The recess could be filled with a mixture of white lead and tallow, making a sticky end to the lead; this process was called arming. The idea was that the lead would pick up a sample of the sea bed, and the line would give a depth. As well as soundings being marked on an Admiralty Chart, there was a fair sprinkling of bottom samples; some Masters used to go almost as much on these samples as on the depth. It has always interested me that the words in the song 'Spanish Ladies' are accurate:

'. . . We got forty-five fathoms and a fine sandy bottom. Then filled our main topsail up Channel to steer.' If an 'Approaches to the English Channel' chart is studied, the information gives a pretty good position.

At lunch, learning that lead-lines had been a morning topic, the Chief Engineer added his own story. It concerned a Master who prided himself on his knowledge of what samples came up on the lead and his prowess in relating it with the ship's position. His two Mates over the months became exasperated with his accuracy. In desperation they sought out the Scots Chief Engineer and scraped the mud off his shore-going boots. The result was presented to the Old Man after the next cast of the lead. The Old Man examined it with horror and shouted, 'Stop engines, let go both anchors! We're aground at the junction of Sauchiehall Street and Argyle Street!' It was the first time I had heard a very old tale, and I have heard it many times since, always with enjoyment.

The hand-lead was never used in anger; when it was dry it went back onto its reel and mercifully stayed there. Any soundings required were taken with the echo-sounder in the chart-room; a continuous concise device which apparently stopped ships running aground in the middle of Glasgow.

Everybody agreed that Sparks had the best job in the ship; he had no work in port. By law he closed the station as the ship entered port and did not reopen it until we were at sea again. He was free in port unless he had any small repairs to do and of course his batteries seemed to need a daily check. This daily check involved clumping around over the Old Man's accommodation and then making loud remarks at breakfast about the batteries being in perfect order. By about half-past nine he would have remarked to the Mate that he was just going ashore for a bit, told the Pantry that he might just not be in for lunch, and just faded; though like Alice's cat he seemed to leave his smile with us.

His hobby, he explained, was travelling as far as possible by train and paying as little as possible for doing it. He went on to point out that everybody wanted to do this, but they all tried to do it for gain.

'Everybody wants to get somewhere without paying. I don't. I want to get there and back without paying with absolutely no objective out there. I have a frame of mind on these trips for which no railway outfit is designed. I always write and thank the railway concerned with a full explanation why, but not how of course, when the ship has sailed. I give them my UK address and nine out of ten outfits reply in the most pleasant vein.'

When I was up for a Second Mate's Certificate in later years I found that travelling home on a Friday brought a choice: pay the fare and have nothing to spend in the bar, or vice versa. Using two of Sparks' devices, I travelled down each weekend for nothing, but the first job on Saturday morning was to send a cheque off to British Rail and square the account. Some months later I had a very nice letter from British Rail thanking me for my patronage, as by my cheques I had travelled regularly from A to B, and would I mind in future paying the fare before I took the journey. So pleasant, in fact, that I have paid my fare in advance ever since.

Sparks was Yoga at sea and a keen railway traveller in port. Others had other interests. The Third Engineer used to disappear into large cars that were sent for him each evening he was not on duty. The cars contained two or three smartly-dressed women; everybody was a bit mystified, because the chap was in his forties and rather unprepossessing ones at that. He explained to me quietly and later in the voyage that he was a champion ballroom dancer in his part of the UK and word spread before him to whichever part of the world he was going to. He showed me pictures of himself, done up in tie and claw-hammer jacket, and I would hardly have recognised him as the same man; other photographs showed medals, cups, sashes, rosettes and whatever else good dancers win. He urged me to take it up as a hobby which gave very good exercise and a lot of friends everywhere.

The mail was arriving fairly regularly, which made all hands contented, although a cynical Hank said he preferred to receive only his racing cuttings; they were more honest and reliable.

The Fourth Engineer was bubbling over one day with news from home about a new litter of Pekingese puppies, which his wife bred as part pets and part business. I was intrigued because we had a young Peke at home which did not seem to be shaping up to a normal dog in behaviour at all. I enquired of the Fourth that evening about Pekes, not letting on that we had one, and his information proved outrageously accurate when I got home and observed ours!

'Bloody things, sit down in blue serge, get up in 'Arris Tweed, that's them.'

'They are usually about two moves ahead of you. If one is lying on the floor doing nothing, give it a lump with your foot; it has either been up to mischief or is contemplating some. Your action cuts it down to only being one move ahead.'

'In a room they always get to the highest and most comfortable place and then observe.'

'My wife and I often laugh and say that the prophet in the Bible who forewarned of the Yellow Peril had just met his first Peke.'

'Bring them up properly as a very hard dog, not a lap dog; they'll teach you the soft side later.'

'Keep them in sight, if they are not they are up to no good.'

'If they are on a lap getting the "coochi-coochi diddums" treatment, watch them; the little sods are not in the least interested in the donor, they are looking round the room choosing who is to be the next candidate for investment.'

'Movement? They don't walk or run, they locomote. Speed? I heard that the Royal Aircraft Establishment ran some tests on a batch over several weeks and their report only read "half a knot faster than the owners!"'

'Above all, let sleeping Pekes lie.'

'They are worse than elephants for memory and persistency.'

This last, some years later I had cause to remember when our own Peke finally cornered a much-watched fox fur. I don't know what sex it was, but it was the quickest change of life a fox fur ever had.

With only the flow of grain down the elevator chutes, the ship was silent during the working day; the sound of our winches thumping and rattling away was noticeable by its absence.

I'd been detailed one morning to give the Second Officer what I hoped was assistance with some of his charts and publications. A nice quiet job in the chartroom and the Second had said to smoke if I wanted to.

Suddenly the noise of sheep was upon us; I looked up in

puzzlement at the Second, who explained smilingly what it was.

'It'll be that Liverpool tramp-ship coming down the dock and our Geordies getting their own back. You've heard the performance put up by every British ship we pass; well, each crowd from a different port always like to niggle crowds from another. This is a classic in its way, because she has a full crowd of North Walians aboard.'

I looked more puzzled.

'At sea, North Wales and South Wales are considered to be utterly different countries. North Wales breeds a lot of sheep, the South does not. What the rest of the Merchant Service always wants to know is how well the North cosset their sheep through the long winter evenings. Everybody pretends to have joyful suspicions, which of course infuriates.'

There were Bahs, Baaaas, Ba Bas, all rising to a crescendo as the other tramp drew abreast of us.

'Open the door and stand well back out of sight. I'll give them a dose with the megaphone from the gloom here; everybody is allowed to join in.'

The Old Man appeared, breathless, from the landward door of the chartroom, and I prepared for a squall.

'Quick, ask them if they have worn their seaboots out,' he ordered, and disappeared.

The ship passed and the noise subsided.

'What's the seaboot angle?' I asked.

'Oh! that's the quickest way to start a fight with a North Walian. Just ask him if he wears seaboots in bed. Sheep in North Wales are very agile.'

In later years the Merchant Service found new soubriquets for the inhabitants of beautiful Wales. They became North Viet Taffs or South Viet Taffs.

The bagged grain started arriving one morning and loading

them into certain spaces was a sign that our stay was drawing to a close. The Mate's tape-measure was much in view to get everything right to begin with. As the Second said, you rarely end up with a ship loaded exactly as planned, but if you are not meticulous in the first instance, you have given yourself little chance.

Towards the end of loading the tape-measure was even more in evidence, as the vessel came down to the mark that the Mate wanted. She sank one inch for every fifty tons loaded. I had thought that a ship just loaded down to the Plimsoll mark and called it a day; but it appeared that several factors were brought into consideration and then an allowance in inches made above or below the mark. The vessel might have a slight list, so both port and starboard marks were measured and the mean taken. This required two sturdy pilot ladders to be placed over each side.

Measuring the inshore mark was tricky. The moorings were slack, and it was a case of waiting until the vessel had drifted off the quay to take a measurement.

On one occasion the Chief Officer was down with his tape; my mate and I were leaning over the rail. I took note of the four-foot gap between ship and quay and could not resist asking, innocently but loudly, of my mate, 'Is she coming in?' I have never seen a man climb a ladder so fast.

In spite of us keeping straight faces, he soon realised the truth. He explained at length, firstly why he thought keel-hauling was too good for me, and secondly what he would do instead, if I tried that sort of trick again. A silly thing to do, really, like calling 'Wolf! Wolf!' too often; but I have still never seen a Chief Officer move so quickly.

After what seemed an age, loading began to be completed. The rather quaint phrase that I had to pass on from the Mate, 'Tell the Bo'sun he can have No 3,' meant that cargo was finished at that hatch and Four Eyes could start operations on it. We got the hatches one by one and battening down was a comparatively leisurely affair; so much so that no hovering stevedores were able to borrow Chippy's precious wedges. The last hatch finished, with much tape-measuring going on by the Mate: we still had to call at Montevideo for bunkers, and he needed a few spare inches for these.

The papers, pilot and tugs arrived. None of the crew were adrift; it's peculiar that seamen never go adrift when the ship is sailing homeward bound from her last loading port! So we sailed amidst the usual barracking from other British ships. Everybody was cheerful; the Cook even began speaking again with Hank for the first time since Christmas.

The Cook had made a really tip-top Christmas cake, but Hank did not like the stuff anyway, so denigration was the order of the day. He had been on deck telling two or three smiling bystanders about it. 'Yes, the Cook got the recipe from Number 617 Squadron, Royal Air Force. You know, the Dambusters. They used to drop things like that on submarine pens and flying-bomb launching sites, they broke the concrete up a treat.'

Unfortunately the Cook had been standing right behind him, so things were quiet between them for many days.

The call at Montevideo seemed obscure to me: I would have thought they had oil in Buenos Aires. On enquiry I was told that it was all down to price, and that we went where it was cheapest.

Passage down the Plate was uneventful. This was always a good thing because on a merchant ship events cost money. Gales, men overboard, sea serpents, civil commotions, Restraint of Princes, and other marine hazards were all very interesting; but all lost money on the 'Venture', which was how the dear old

Company still described a round voyage.

We were steaming down the channel for Montevideo. Out of the haze appeared the wreck of a ship, but not a normal ship; then I remembered that she must be the *Graf Spee*. Chippy was nearby, glowering at the remains of the ship that had caused havoc amongst British shipping during the war.

'Pocket battleships we called them, the Germans classed them as *Panzerschiffe* or Armoured Ship; there were three of them altogether and one of the bastards sank the ship I was on, and put me in a prison camp for five years,' Chippy almost snarled. Then his face lightened as he went on: 'She was alright sinking merchant ships, but she got herself mixed up with three British cruisers. Aye, *Exeter* and *Ajax* from the Royal Navy with *Achilles* from the Royal New Zealand Navy; they certainly pissed on her matches. As you know, she reached Montevideo and a day or two later came out and scuttled herself where you see her.' It is not possible to describe a wreck as menacing or ominous, but there was an air about her that was different from any other I have ever seen.

Chippy went on to describe his capture and the journey across most of Europe to a place that nobody had heard of before and apparently never wished to hear of again.

'So there we were, about five hundred of us, right back in the middle of nowhere. We'd been reminded that, with our civilian status as merchant seamen, any of us found wandering about in Germany would be shot.

'The cigarette supply was very good. The booze side took a bit longer as we had to make it ourselves, but it was not many weeks before we had a passable brew going and it improved as we learned. So it was a case of sitting tight and waiting for the war to end. It never seriously occurred to any of us that we could actually lose, particularly after being messed about the way we had been.

'Anyway, come Christmas, we had a party one evening. The guards were down to one in the compound and they did five-hour watches for some reason. My hut had not long started its party when everybody noticed that the new guard was the most disliked of all. Well, you know what seamen are, as a drink takes hold.

'"The Rotten Bastard."

'"I bet he's bloody cold, I hope."

'"Well, he's only the worst of not a bad lot."

'"He's away from home for Christmas."

'"I wonder if he's got a wife and kids."

'"It's colder than usual tonight, he'll be bloody cold by the end of his watch."

'"He's not a bad bastard really."

'"Well, it is Christmas."

'"Invite the poor old sod in for a quick one."

'So in he came, and of course, it wasn't long before a quickie became two and so on. Anyway, not being used to our plonk, he collapsed. There was the problem that halfway through his watch he had to go to the gate which was near our hut and report. We had noted that it was always the same question and always the guards only replied, "*Ja, mein Stugelflugel,*" or some such. So we stripped his uniform off him, found one of the A.B.s that it fitted and dressed him in German gear. He didn't like the idea at all, but once we had him dressed it was OK. We said we were going to chuck him out anyway, and if he was found in the compound when we raised the alarm, as we would if he didn't at least try, he would probably get shot. A dummy run with the slung rifle, he would only lazily have to touch the breach in a mild salute. A quick time check, then he was out in the snow on his own.

'He did the job perfectly, shambled over to the gate, saluted, said "*Ja, mein Stugelfugel*," and came back. It took him about four minutes in all, and was he thirsty when he got back!

'By the end of the watch we had the German sobered up and redressed. Then we pushed him out into the snow to go for his relief.'

'How about the War Effort?' I asked. 'That didn't seem to help it much.'

'War Effort?' said Chippy indignantly. 'What do you mean War Effort? It was a merchant navy camp and we were just keeping the bloody job going. The poor bastard might have got the sack for being pissed on watch!'

Bunkering in Montevideo was just a case of anchoring in the harbour and loading from a barge; with the Chief Officer doing his tape-measure stunts for the last time. All this measuring was rather vital; an inch too much and the law was being broken for overloading, but an inch too little meant the loss of fifty tons freight.

As far as we were concerned, the most important news was that we were to go on wheel watches for the passage home. This would release two A.B.s from the watch system, who would work on deck all day instead. The mate obviously reckoned he would get more work out of the two seamen, and they could not complain because he would just say we needed the experience. We were to go on separate watches, the twelve-to-four and the four-to-eight.

For leaving Montevideo, I presented myself at the wheel. I was asked by the Old Man if I had been on the wheel before, in and out of port. My negative reply was answered by; 'I don't want a first-timer on the wheel. Get a relief.'

As I made my way down from the bridge I wondered how, if I was never allowed to take a ship in or out of port to start with, I would ever be able to say that I had!

It proved the same with different ships and Masters throughout the rest of my time. The first time I took the wheel was during a shift in Manchester docks as a newly promoted Third Mate; it never occurred to the Master to ask his Third Officer about his wheel experience! We did the shift with a shore gang of riggers who did not provide a wheelman, so at last my chance came. The only drawback was that I had the whistle, telephones, telegraphs and movement book to look after as well, so the much-hallowed wheel spent most of its time jammed in various positions by some flags which were handy. But never ever did I take a ship in and out of port as an indentured apprentice!

Still, no matter, being on the wheel during a stand-by was not necessarily a happy job. A short stand-by could well develop into a long one and everybody could easily forget the poor old wheelman; dying for a smoke, bursting for a pee, and probably frozen stiff because both wheelhouse doors were open and the place was like a wind-tunnel with hiccups.

I had been taught to steer outward-bound; not much to it in fine weather once, like all beginners, I learned not to 'chase the compass' or put on too much wheel. I had steered small craft both by tiller and wheel on compass courses, with success that had occasioned diminishingly fewer lumps on the skull, as dissatisfaction was shown in my part of the world. Ocean-going ships needed a less catholic approach, I found. Curiously enough, the army dodgers were quite good at it; Hank explained that the laziest men always make the best helmsmen because unconsciously it would be in their make-up to work the wheel as little as possible.

The magnetic steering compass was treated with great respect. Being on the wheel was the one place of duty to which a seaman took no knife; it might upset the compass. Officers wore brass buttons on uniform jackets, not for smartness, but because that metal would not affect the compass when they were using it. A large brass buckle on a belt aroused no comment, but a wheelman arriving on the bridge with a heavy steel one was sent straight off to swap it for a piece of rope yarn. If Chippy turned up with his tool-bag he was watched carefully to see that he did not get too near the sacred compass. Probably it was an over-precaution, but no visible chance was taken. I was not allowed on the wheel as a first-time learner until I had disposed of my knife and when I came off, the Mate, who had been inspecting it, said it was wrong anyway. I had a point on it, which could be used for stabbing, so I was sent for'd to Chippy and his grindstone to have the end removed. I then had a knife with a so-called Board of Trade point, which, as Chippy pointed out, could be used as a handy screw-driver in any case.

The actual navigation was done from the standard compass on the next deck up, the Monkey Island, and the course checked down to the steering. The steering compass was a dry-card compass which in bad weather could swing like a bastard. The standard compass had its bowl filled with liquid which caused a blessed dampening effect. The liquid was a mixture of alcohol and distilled water: this was chiefly as an anti-freeze.

Some years later I joined a ship as Second Officer, and, during the handover, the officer I was relieving stressed the fact that the standard compass bowl had a bubble in it and was to go ashore for repair, but not before the Chief Officer had seen me. This was strange. The Second Officer acted under the Master as far as navigational equipment went, and it was no real business of the Mate to interfere, particularly as he was ashore for several hours. It was only because the Chief Officer was a very old friend of mine that I did not let the compass go with the Nautical Optician when he called for other gear.

On the Chief Officer's return he dashed into my cabin and the first greeting I got from the old friend was: 'Have you let that bloody compass go ashore?' I pointed to the corner where it was and he looked quite relieved, suggested tea and that we would see about the compass that evening, when things had quietened down for the day. Later he crept into my cabin with a screwdriver, a new plastic bucket, and an explanation. They'd tried everything to get rid of the bubble without success and as a last resort he and the Old Man had emptied it fully one evening during the Mate's watch, refilling it with gin.

So that evening we worked behind a locked door emptying the compass bowl into the bucket. We got a bottle each from the operation. The idea of smuggled spirits had not crossed his mind, but to get two free bottles of gin out of the Company was of paramount importance to him. We agreed, while drinking the rebottled gin, that it didn't taste in the least magnetic!

Being on the wheel was boring in fine weather with no traffic to alter for. The relief of the wheel was not necessarily so, particularly if I found myself on the middle watch with Jan and Deaf Charlie. Receiving the wheel from Jan was ear-screwing; I would get from him, for example, 'Ootsven tak woanafstif.' This would need checking over before I was quite sure that he meant the course and wheel movement was 'Oh Two Seven, taking one-and-a-half turns of starboard wheel.'

Charlie was different: he couldn't hear and I couldn't shout because that would have disturbed the watch officer or woken the Old Man. It had to be done in sign language, in the dark. Goodness alone knows how they ever handed over to each other. I was just glad I was not there at the time; probably braille was used!

As well as a great Flags and Lights Company, we were also apparently a great Bell Company. Ship's time in Bells was, I suspect, invented originally to confuse landsmen. Shortly after I went to sea somebody somewhere realised that landsmen were confused enough in matters nautical without adding Bells to their bewilderment.

Bells is quite simple, really.

There are six four-hour watches in a day. Bells was made, rung or struck for each watch period only. Hence Bells mark a four-hour passage of time. Eight to end the previous and start the new watch, and then every half-hour in increasing numbers from one to seven.

Jan told me that in the Navy it was roughly the same, 'Except they have things called Dogwatches which seem to have something to do with time off, but I never listen properly because what the Navy does with its pets in its spare time has nothing to do with me.'

Bells was operated through the day on the small wheelhouse bell, which was connected to the helmsman by a length of line and at night answered by the lookout on the fo'c's'le head where the large ship's bell was. So at one o'clock in the morning, two half-hours having passed, it was ding-dong by the wheelhouse and an answering dong-dong from forrard.

The Company being an old-fashioned one, nobody seemed to be used to the idea that we had electric navigation lights with alarms on the bridge. So the lookout was still in the days of oil lamps and continued reporting with a lusty hail, 'Lights are bright.' The Officer of the Watch, custom ordained, had to answer with a slow bored lusty hail of: 'Aye, aye.'

It was not too bad at the beginning of the watch, but towards the end of the watch with six or seven bells being rung it all began to sound like a marshalling yard in an American railway film. No wonder the poor bloody albatross stayed away during the night!

It was found that in a cross wind of about three or four upwards, a cry of 'You're full of shite,' or 'Can I ride your bike,' would still get the long, bored response of 'Aye, aye.' The ultimate was to wait until the wind was a good force five, then:

'Ding, ding.'

'Dong, dong.'

'Can I unfrock your wife?'

'Aye, aye.'

Childish it may be thought; but for a seventeen-year old apprentice to be shouting that sort of thing up to the mighty Second Officer meant living in great danger.

Things had changed by the time I became Third Officer, and I never had the chance of ending the exchange by giving a lusty hail of 'Piss Off!' Nobody would have noticed anyway, I expect.

The main function of the lookout forward was to report any lights, be they of ship or shore. One stroke of the bell if the light was to starboard, two to port, and three for dead ahead. It was not unknown for lookouts to ring up for low-rising planets or the moon. Irishmen were always supposed to ring the moon up anyway and for that reason it was often referred to among seamen as 'Paddy's Lantern'. Naturally nothing was ever said from the bridge about these mistakes; it was much better to have too much reported than too little.

Being on the wheel was incredibly boring once one had learned to steer, unless the watch officer felt chatty. The Second Mate was excellent value, particularly about wartime experiences.

'. . . Everything happened so fast. Misrecognition was by no means unknown. I remember being one of three British merchantmen that were attacked by the Royal Air Force. Luckily some German fighters turned up and drove them off. Mind you, we had to get the bloody Red Ensigns down pretty quickly in case the Jerries flew back over low for a vote of thanks.'

'. . . One of the anti-aircraft weapons looked roughly like an army three-inch mortar; it could be far more lethal. The idea was to fire a hand-grenade at passing aircraft, using compressed air if you were a motor ship, or steam if you were a steamer. This was called a Holman projector. I'm told that on motor ships the apparatus projected alright because compressed air had to come at regular pressure. I was only in steamers with them, where the Chief Engineers regarded the dear old projector as just another deck appliance that wasted their steam. Consequently the steam line to it was only cracked open. We used to find that a crew of two worked it best. One to load, train, elevate and fire; the other to catch the grenade when it just cleared the barrel and throw the bloody thing overboard.'

Some of Jan's wartime comments were incredible; always being made with his deadpan face, of course.

'. . . After the Occupation of Holland I found the British Merchant Service. Before that I was in Combined Operations with the Dutch to hunt submarines. They give me a rowing boat and a pot of black paint and send me up the coast. They follow ashore with a mobile anti-aircraft gun. When I see a submarine periscope I paint it black and the skipper not being able see starts to rise; when he's risen to five hundred feet the AA gun shoot him down. It never worked because they kept forgetting to give me a paint brush.'

'. . . three days afloat on a piece of oily waste.'

'. . . the narrow-gutted old bastard. Roll? We had to put a net over the funnel to keep the fireman in.'

'. . . four weeks adrift in an open-necked shirt.'

'She was very old ship, built as sister ship to Noah's Ark, I think. They put wire netting all underneath to keep the fish out.'

Deaf Charlie had observations about wartime.

'I'd had something to do with the Navy when I was young, and the fact always got out although it was not noted in my Discharge Book. As a result I always got put on the after-gun;

most ships carried a twelve-pounder, you can see the strengthening around the poop house on this ship if you look. The damn things used to go off with such a crack, so we were issued with ear plugs. This move was not really successful as the first bang used to blow the bloody plugs out! Subsequent shots used to be painful on the ears. I'm certain that's what caused me to go so deaf. Anyway, the Pool doctor is always very understanding when I tell him that I hear better once away at sea, particularly now there are no guns going off.'

'Getting recalled from leave was often a bit unusual; it involved the police in a lot of cases. Just To Make Sure The Message Had Got Through. Far different from pre-war days when if you had had a good trip with a good pay-off you stayed at home until you got a Discharge Book breakfast.'

'What's a Discharge Book breakfast?' I enquired. The book in question was a record, stamped up ship by ship, as a Merchant Seaman onward progressed, but I had never heard it connected with food before.

'When your wife considered the time had come, you sat down at table for breakfast and all you got was your Discharge Book on a plate in front of you. That meant she thought it was time you went back to sea.'

'What did you say the first time you received that sort of meal?' I asked.

'I told her the plate was cold. There was a silent pause, and then she hit me over the head with an iron colander, the daft bitch. Luckily she drew blood, otherwise our marriage might have failed. Next trip I saved like mad and bought her all light aluminium cooking gear to be on the safe side; but I still think the wartime message via the law was guaranteed to be less painful.'

One morning an A.B. reported to the Chief Steward with

toothache, a filling having fallen out. An empty tooth can be nothing or lethal. The A.B.'s was lethal. The Shipmaster's Medical Guide really could not be expected to cover too much dentistry. Nevertheless, the committee formed itself and during the afternoon the Old Man decided on treatment. Chippy was dispatched for'd to his shop for a little oakum and told to tease it well. The Mate was dispatched to his locker for a small tin of plastic wood. He looked surprised and resentful that anybody, even the ship's Master, should have knowledge of what was stowed in the depths of Fort Knox.

The patient, on appearing in the evening, said that he felt much better, but the wheels of Dental Science were in motion and he stood no chance. A quick wash round the mouth with whisky, with a second just to remove the trace of the previous, and the treatment was on. A small plug of oakum was placed in the cavity and was gently thrust home with somebody's finger. A suggestion that Chippy should bang it in with his caulking mallet was ignored. The next step was a plug of plastic wood placed atop by somebody else's finger, so that hygiene was always observed.

To everybody's lasting bewilderment, the treatment worked perfectly. It was rather an anti-climax when the A.B. returned, properly stopped, from the first available dentist, with a report that the previous plug-up had been quite clever. Apparently oakum has funny properties that make it as good for placing in internal ivory as it is for banging into wooden decks.

Four Eyes said that in desperate straits he had removed one of his own teeth with a pair of mole grips; I can well believe it, he was that sort of person.

The ruling for short dental treatment was simple. If an extraction was required, the Company paid; but any stoppings, fillings or other repairs came out of a man's wages. It sounded a bit harsh, but under another system you might well have ended up with half the crowd having treatment half the time. Who would be the first one to ask for gold fillings, for nothing? Any obviously genuine filling and stopping, such as our seaman's, usually got called an extraction, providing that it was a one-visit-and-finish job. Nothing was ever said, but he would just find that there was no deduction on his pay-off slip.

With someone's birthday coming up at home, I went to Sparks in the Radio Room which, with his cabin, was situated on the bridge. He called it the Radio Room; other radio officers might call it their office, but to everybody else it was known as 'Sparkie's Shack'. When radios were first placed aboard existing ships, before and during the First World War, the equipment was housed in a wooden lean-to structure on a boat-deck near the Bridge, and the term Shack was coined and had stuck.

I was sent down to ask the Old Man, whose radio station it was; Sparks was the operator on his behalf. I was slightly put out by having to go and get permission from the Old Man: it smelled of some sort of censorship. The Second Mate, on my tactful enquiry later, explained that it was purely financial in reason: It would be very easy to run up a large radio account. The Old Man knew how much money people had in the ship; Sparks did not. As the Second asked me to imagine, what would happen if Hank suddenly decided to go horse-racing by radio telegram? He could run up a large bill in no time at all.

On returning to the Shack, I was presented with three alternative ways to send a message to the UK. The first was a straight telegram. The second was cheaper but took longer, it was known as a 'Ship's Letter Telegram', SLT for short. This went by radio as a telegram to the usual receiving station at Portishead, but was transmitted onwards as a letter through the post. The third way, which nobody ever used because it seemed rather unlikely, was to radio the message to the nearest homeward-bound mail steamer; the assumption was that she would post it as a letter when she docked. I selected an SLT for my purpose and Sparks said he would get it away next watch. Radio messages never seemed to have been sent, they were always 'Got Away'.

Sparks worked through fourteen hours of the day in two-hour watches, with a break of two hours between each watch. Add to this the fact that he worked on GMT, while the ship's time altered with longitude, and it meant he was usually out of step with the rest of us. His schedule did change so that he did not have to work all night, but nevertheless it called for some early mornings and late evenings. He was in the ship predominantly as a safety factor in case of distress calls by us or other ships, but obviously the owners found it handy to communicate with the ship if anything cropped up, and particularly in our case where we were still waiting for news of our port of discharge.

We had loaded grain for discharge UK/Continent. On leaving the Plate there was an apparent host of destinations, but I got clever and had an illicit look at the Deck Log Book while I had business in the chart-room. At the top of the page it clearly stated that we were bound from Montevideo to Lefo. At the next short break my mate and I made a dive for our atlases and other reference books to find the whereabouts of Lefo; we had no success whatsoever.

Chatting to the Fourth Engineer brought little further information. 'Yes, the Third and I have both looked at the Chief's Engine Room Log Book; the Second Steward has had a boggle at the fair copy of the Deck Log while the Mate has had it out to copy up to date. Nobody has heard of the bloody place. Even old Ali, the Fireman, who has been at sea since James Watt was a donkey-greaser, just shakes his head. We all think it must be on the outskirts of some large port and is not normally known by the name, but we cannot ask, otherwise we'll be accused of prying.'

The Chief Steward helped solve the conundrum of approach to authority. 'When you two are on the bridge this afternoon, pick a moment and innocently ask what goes in the Log Book when the destination is uncertain.'

The Second Mate smiled when asked. 'You nosey young bastards have been snuffling in that Log Book for two days now, wondering where Lefo is, I have no doubt. In the days before radio in steamships, and certainly during the days of sail, many bulk cargoes changed ownership on the way home, depending on the market requirement; consequently they made for the nearest UK coastal telegraph station where they could pick up orders visually by flag or light signalling. Lefo is not a port; it stands for "Land's End For Orders". I asked the Old Man if I should put UK/Continent in the Log Book and on the Chief's daily chit, but he just wanted Lefo to keep people curious.' It was just another Captain-type leg-pull which none of us thought very funny. We apparently would get orders by radio long before Land's End.

Sparks also had Lefo in his log book, but almost anything to do with radio traffic was secret. Even the weather forecasts and navigational warnings he received were confidential; some masters would require to see them before giving permission for them to be put on the bridge for many to see.

'Our orders will come before long, and they will be a secret between me and the Old Man. It will be no use anybody creeping in here looking at my Radio Log for the answer; messages as such are not written in, only the details of their passage. I keep a carbon copy usually, but on this occasion I'll take him the carbon as well, just to prove I'm legitimate. I hope the old bastard doesn't sit on it for too long, as it will be difficult for me to keep it secret by word or gesture, because I am not even allowed to let on that the vital message has arrived; even though everybody will sense it.'

A few days later Sparks took to his adjoining cabin and shack one morning and would only come out and down below for his lavatorial arrangements late at night when nobody was about. On the excuse of radio traffic that was difficult, he had basic meals sent up to him.

The message had arrived. The Old Man was sitting on it.

This was a desperate time. If bound for the UK, it meant that the voyage ended after five-and-a-half months and the crew paid off to go on leave. If, on the other hand, the ship was going to the continent, she would sail outward with no pay-off and eighteen months of the Articles still to run. The information was of great import to us all and yet there was the Old Man keeping it to himself. Did he think it funny? I do not know, I only know that we thought it stank.

On the evening of the second day, Hank went to the Chief Steward with a gambling suggestion. Later in the evening they grabbed Sparks on his way back from the bathroom and took him into the Chief Steward's cabin and shut the door. Next day at breakfast, the Mate told the Old Man that the Chief Steward had made up a sweep amongst the crew for the destination and mentioned that he had been put in for a couple of ports and wanted the money.

The sweep was posted up on the notice board at morning smokoe. The Old Man, finding himself due to win the second prize, went onto the Bridge at noon and announced to all in hearing that the vessel was ordered to Liverpool. The news flashed around the ship, its progress easily marked by bouts of cheering. The Old Man went and picked up his second prize from the Chief Steward.

It must have been about the phoniest sweep ever produced. Hank and the Chief Steward and Sparks and a rum bottle and the ports of the sweep had got all mixed together; the resultant draw gave the Old Man the second prize. Hank told me several days later that Sparks had not actually given the game away as such, just helped with the ports that he didn't think we were going to; a fair amount of rum and persuasion assisted. If they had let the Old Man win, he'd have smelled a rat. The first prize and third prize did not exist, and nobody in the ship had been asked if they wanted to join the sweep. So it really boiled down to Hank and the Chief paying out a few bob to the Old Man, just to give him a nudge and spill the beans.

The ship's company became very joyful with the information, the exception being Four Eyes, who still had to get some work out of the deck crowd. He said to me, mournfully, 'We have now entered the "Kiss My Arse Latitudes".'

The Chief Cook got rather unjoyful and stayed that way for a day or so. One of the army dodgers had, in his hearing, referred to the impending curry as 'Duck Shite and Hailstones.'

Jan got over-joyful, came off the wheel and went to see the Chief Steward. A few minutes later there was a roar of laughter from Jan and a howl of rage from the Chief Steward. Jan walked past one or two of us who were standing on deck and made his way aft with tears of laughter on his face. A few minutes later an annoyed Chief Steward joined our group; someone asked him what was wrong.

'It's that mangle-tongued bloody A.B. He came into my cabin and pulled the door curtain after him, walked across to where I was sitting, opened his flies and flopped his wedding tackle onto my desk, then gazed at me in mute appeal. I picked up a pencil and poked it, and squeezed it; I looked at it through a magnifying glass, then sat back and asked, "What's wrong with it?"

"Nothing," he said, "but isn't it a beauty?"

'Of all the bung-faced . . .' The rest was drowned by our laughter.

The radio-outward traffic picked up with the telegrams and SLTs of the many who wanted to inform their loved ones of the expected arrival in Liverpool. Sparks was much happier with something to do, and often spent periods into his off-watch time getting messages away. His was a fairly boring job, sitting and listening to Morse code day in, day out. Occasionally he would find another ship to chat to over the ether. What was said? Who knows. I was amused, however, to discover that sparkies have their own unofficial Morse sign to denote a laugh!

He was a pleasant old chap, but he warned against his profession.

'I seem to have come through alright; unfortunately, many sparkies become a bit strange after too long at sea. Some say it is the Morse that does it; I think differently. You have seen by now that ship-board life is indescribably different in attitude from that ashore. Take the fact that a radio officer's job is completely different from that of any of his shipmates; this makes him almost doubly different from anything ashore, and consequently the lonely Sparks is, in a lot of cases, bound to start thinking along lines which nobody else does.'

One of the things which alleviated boredom aboard was the ship's library. This consisted of about one hundred assorted books, and the Third Officer acted as librarian. One of the troubles with a ship's library is that people will not bring the books back as soon as they have finished them; they wait until they require something else to read before the return. This means that someone will take a library book and read it, then sit on it until he happens to have finished two or three paperbacks which he has up his sleeve, which may take weeks.

The library was provided each trip by an outfit called the Seafarer's Education Service, and was changed each voyage. Changes abroad could be made between ships, provided detailed lists were sent off to the SES by both parties. The SES would provide any book that was asked for in the library; in later ships I sailed in, where crews returned regularly, it was quite the thing for the librarian to go round halfway through the voyage asking which books were required in the next lot. They would arrive in boxes of fifty each, when the new books were placed on the shelves and the old ones sent off in the boxes, often within the hour. I have always felt a bit sorry for the boxes: the books might have some peace and quiet at each end; the poor old boxes were on the go non-stop. I have always wondered what their average life was, because anything that gets carried on and off ships gets an incredible battering.

On the way home I had exhausted the library and looked around for something to read. The Second Officer carried his own set of books with him, all well-known books of the sea, of the type that can be read and re-read with pleasure. The miserable bastard would not lend them at all! He stuck to the old superstition that it was unlucky to lend books about the sea. Two others he had I was allowed to borrow with pleasure, but his nautical books, no!

Wedges around a hatch were always of paramount importance, even the way they were faced. You could have all the King and Queen beams, all the tarpaulins, all the hatch boards and all the battens, but it was the wedges that kept it all finally secured in place.

Hatch wedges were placed with the blunt end facing forward; this was on the assumption that anything breaking adrift, or any heavy water, would be travelling from forward to aft, and if the wedges were hit they would be driven further in rather than knocked completely out. After a few days of baking-hot weather, one of Chippy's jobs was to go round and check that none of the wedges were slack through having dried out too much. Of course, entering any bad weather meant that the wedges were wetted and they tightened themselves snugly on their own.

In the same way, the top tarpaulin of the three used on each hatch was always the oldest, and when this got a bit damp it tautened and held the other two stiffly. Heavy seas hit all sorts of things in ships and happily do no damage when there is no movement in the objects; the sea quickly finds anything loose or slightly moveable and troubles start.

If you left a port and a sudden gale sprang up it was attributed easily. In the saloon the remark was, 'Somebody has not paid their laundry bill'. The same person on deck would re-phrase the remark to, 'Some bastard hasn't paid their bloody whore!'

However, we had been out of port for a long time and there was nothing sudden about the gale we hit off the Bay. The old rhyme:

> Long foretold, long last;
> Short notice, soon past,

applied with its first part, as the barometer slowly dropped and the wind steadily increased to force ten and stayed there for too long in everybody's opinion.

The barometer reading was noted in the deck log book every hour instead of the customary four hours. It got lower and lower; a couple of times I heard the Old Man remark, 'I think the bottom has fallen out of the bloody thing!'

The wind increased from the south-west, which put it on our port quarter, and with it sea and swell. Steering became more difficult, with more frequent wheel movements. Any wheel movement was transmitted by two thin hydraulic pipes half the length of the ship to the steam-driven steering engine which actually turned the rudder. The steering engine compartment was adjacent to the sailors' sleeping accommodation and that was why, in normal times, a wheelman steered with as few wheel movements as possible: excessive steering engine noise irritated the watches below and caused complaints. The complaints did not go through any official channels: they went direct from the crowd to the wheelman when he came off watch! However, with the weather becoming heavier on the quarter, the steering engine was working almost continuously.

The weather became more unpleasant through the night, with the ship rolling and pitching in consequence. It was hard to tell the difference between spray and rain, and my mate suggested that it would not really matter if we did not bother further, as it all seemed to be equally wet. We were mopping up the wheelhouse, chart-room and Sparkie's shack, which seemed to accumulate water from nowhere, when the Mate came up about the middle of the forenoon watch for a yarn with the Old Man. There was talk of possible 'pooping', that is shipping heavy water over the stern; no seaman likes the idea as such an occurrence usually causes damage somewhere, and with the crowd living aft, life and limb could be at stake.

The upshot was that my mate was despatched to the Chief Engineer, with the Old Man's compliments, and the advice that the ship would be turned and heave to in about ten minutes. I was sent by the Mate to warn the Chief Steward, Bo'sun and Carpenter to expect heavy rolling as we turned through the swell.

A little later, on return to the bridge, the Third Mate told us to get the NUC balls ready on the Monkey Island and to hoist them up the Christmas Tree when ordered.

The engine room telegraph was rung to 'stand-by' and with the jangled answer from the engine room came the Old Man's instructions to the wheelman to be ready to put the wheel hard-a-port as quickly as possible on demand. Picking his moment, the Old Man gave the order for the helm to be put hard over and after a short delay the ship started swinging rapidly; we got round with only one big roll.

Heaving to with a loaded steamship is a fairly simple manoeuvre, providing everything behaves itself. Once the turn was made, the engines were rung to 'Slow Ahead'.

At slow speeds our propeller, apart from edging us ahead, would give a right-angled effect, as if it were a paddle-wheel, to the ship's stern. This was something called 'transverse thrust', so the Second Mate explained. In our case the fact that the propeller was right-handed would cause the vessel's stern to go to starboard and therefore the bow to go to port. The whole scheme, he explained, was to put the wind fine onto the port bow, so she would tend to blow off to starboard, but the paddle-wheel effect of the propeller would counteract the tendency and keep her bow up to port. She would then be lying almost head-to-wind and sea, nearly stopped in the water, and the minimum of helm use would keep her there; she would just ride up and down comparatively gently over the massive swells, in no way trying to force her way into sea or swell. She behaved herself very well and lay hove-to nicely.

We were then in a state which was known as 'Not Under Command', and this meant that we could not give way to other ships, as we would do in normal circumstances. To signal this fact, the Third Mate ordered us to hoist the prepared NUC balls up the Christmas Tree. These were two basket-made black balls, two feet in diameter, and separated on the halyard by a length of line six feet long and would indicate to other vessels that, if they were on a collision course with us, the shuttlecock was in their court as far as giving way was concerned. They would have to be rather nippy, though, because visibility was well below a quarter of a mile. The two black balls would be replaced by two red lights when darkness came. With the visibility as low as it was, the lookout in each deck watch was maintained by a rating or one of us cadets as in the hours of darkness. The man on stand-by had plenty of odd jobs such as mopping up wheelhouse and chart-room decks and cleaning blocked bridge scuppers.

With the ship riding as well as was possible, shipping tons of spray but only occasional heavy water, there seemed a bit more time to think. The catering staff thought, and realised that the Third Mate had not had a cup of morning coffee. A catering boy appeared with some and tried to climb the open ladder to the bridge; halfway up, the force ten wind, funnelling through between the bridge decks, caught him and blew cup, saucer, spoon and coffee away; we had seen this happen before, because the boys never seemed to realise when there was a wind blowing. What was novel on this occasion was that it blew the boy away as well; my mate and myself were sent to pick him out of his scupper and help him down below. A second attempt by another cabin boy proved more successful: he came up the ladder backwards and reached the top with cup, saucer and spoon intact, but unfortunately all the coffee had blown away. The Third Mate kindly intimated that he did not want any coffee anyway.

Next to appear was the Second Steward bearing a cloth-covered bucket. He turned back to wind and sat on the second step of the ladder, then brought his feet up to the first, clutching the bucket, pumped his arse onto the third step and withdrew his feet to the second; clever stuff, and step by step he reached the top. A short round of applause would have been in order, I felt, for such a masterful performance. Undoing the cloth from the top of his bucket, he produced a mug of steaming coffee and some unsodden biscuits for the Old Man. One obviously did not get to Second Steward in the British Merchant Service without learning some tricks of the trade.

In a larger-crewed ship, the Old Man would have had an Assistant Steward appointed to look to his needs, and that steward would have been known as the Captain's Tiger. In our ship the Second Steward acted as Tiger, amongst his other duties. Whatever the arrangement, Captain's Tigers are aware that in times of stress the Old Man must have his food where he wants it, when he normally has it, and it must be hot and well presented. Tigers will often go to any lengths and certainly beyond the call of duty to achieve the end. Tigers know that, by keeping the Old Man happy in the middle of a gale from a food point of view, they are doing just as much for the ship as at least any one watch of seamen.

Later in the day I was look-out on the starboard wing of the bridge; there was no question of having a lookout forward in that kind of weather. Over the noise of wind rain and spray, I heard the Old Man's raised voice, which ran on for a fair time. I could see through the wheelhouse window that he was screaming at Jan who was on the wheel. I wondered what the matter could be, as Jan was probably the most experienced wheelman in the ship.

When the watch ended, I enquired of Jan what the upset was over. Things had been very quiet after in the wheelhouse with the Old Man and the Watch Officer saying little.

'Captain,' Jan had said, 'I hear just now on the radio that there is a woman raped every three minutes in New York.'

'Really?' the Old Man had answered coldly.

'Yes,' Jan had gone on. 'And she says that she is getting fed up with it.'

That was when the Old Man had exploded.

'What the hell did you say a stupid thing like that for?' I asked.

'Well,' Jan said slowly, 'things were too quiet and the Old Man naturally worried about the situation, so I thought it would do him good to let off steam at somebody. It gives him something else to think about besides the weather, over which he has no control. I must say I did not know he would let off that much steam; he was very impressive!'

Approaching midnight, I was called to go on watch again. I had been farmer on the previous watch so it was my first wheel, and while dressing in the day cabin I was a bit apprehensive. The amount of weather noise was still the same, and when I got my second call the AB came in with oilskins streaming; he remarked that the sky was clear so there would be no rain, but I would not know by going outside, because the flying spray was more than compensating.

On relieving the wheel I was given the course, and told she was taking about two-and-a-half turns of port wheel to maintain it. The Third and Second Officers and the Old Man were in the wheelhouse to start with, but the Third left as soon as he had handed over to the Second. The Old Man went on to explain to the Second Mate that during the previous watch the expected cold front had arrived, and this accounted for the sky clearing; also the barometer had started to rise, which was a good sign, but, he quoted, 'First Rise After Low Foretells Stronger Blow,' and mumbled that the wind was increasing.

Surprisingly enough, there seemingly was not much to steering; two-and-a-half turns on, and then ease to one-and-a-half. Later I found she needed three turns, and not long after that, hard-over.

A short time passed and I had to report, 'Wheel hard-a-port, Sir, and she is not answering.'

'Full ahead,' the Old Man ordered the Second. Gradually the

lubber line on the compass crept back to its correct position on the compass card.

'Slow ahead,' called the Old Man, who had been watching the compass, 'then ring the Engine Room and ask them to put the revolutions up six over the normal slow-ahead figure, and we'll see how that suits her.'

Then to me he said, 'From not on, each time you find you have to use full helm to keep your course, let me know; then I'll just increase speed to make sure she answers. We can't afford to fall off into the trough in this weather.'

'Falling off into the trough' meant getting beam-on to wind, sea and swell, and in the circumstances it would be a dangerous thing to allow to happen, as she would try and roll her guts out. As the Old Man said, we all knew the cargo had been stowed as nearly perfectly as possible, but grain was a funny cargo to play unnecessary games with, and a shifted cargo was everybody's pet nightmare.

So it went on; the ship bucketing around like a bull with its tail shut in a gate, but with the Old Man adjusting the speed until he was satisfied that I only needed to use about three turns of the wheel to keep the ship's head where he wanted it. When hove to, enough engine revs must be used to keep steerage way, but too much speed can cause the vessel to pitch excessively. Too great a degree of pitching causes the screw to clear the water and the engines to race; also the bow can clear the water to an extent when the fore part of the vessel's flat bottom is exposed to fresh air, and when the bow returns to its native element it does so with a hell of a bang. The bang is technically known as 'pounding' and it damages plates which cost money to repair. As I have already explained, anything which cost money on a tramp-ship was very unpopular.

During the second hour of my wheel, one of two small safety

lamps chose its time to jump out of its obviously too-shallow rack and hit me on the head. It did not fall very far before striking me, but when it did, it managed to do so with a sharp corner exactly at the point where the Third Officer had drawn blood earlier in the voyage with the corner of his clip-board. It banged its way into a corner of the wheelhouse, where the Second fielded it and stuffed it into a locker. He knew that I had been hit, by my language, and asked if I was alright. I said that I was alright: the blow was literally sharp, rather than heavy; but I knew that when I went below and inspected things I would find that blood had been drawn.

The crown of my head had always been a bit delicate since my school days, when I had suffered under a tyrannical and brutal French master, an amazing man in two ways: firstly, that he managed to speak French without his normal broad Yorkshire accent; anybody who wanted to mix it had only to hint that his French was easier to understand than his English. Secondly, he had his own way of keeping order. He had a knot in the end of his right gown sleeve and enclosed in the knot was a ball-bearing. For any detected misbehaviour the first knowledge of the detection was a sharp crack on the crown of the head from his innocent-looking gown sleeve, delivered from behind. Purists said that he altered the weight of the ball-bearing according to what age class he was going to teach. Anyway, I ended up with a lot of unsolicited French, but with an Achilles' crown, and if the Merchant Service was going to hit me over the head with clip-boards and drop safety lamps on it, I would have to think of some more gentle employ.

You should not really think while you are on the wheel. The next time the Old Man said, 'How's your head?' I answered, very unthinkingly, 'Alright, Sir, the lamp only fell a few inches.'

The Old Man made a dive at the compass binnacle while

shouting at me, 'Not your head, you stupid little bastard, I mean the ship's head. Of all the idiotic bloody . . .' and so on until he ran out of steam. I consoled myself that I had probably helped him as much as Jan had the previous day.

It was pleasant to get off the wheel for an hour before standing the final hour of the watch as lookout. The final hour spent on the wing of the bridge was just wet and cold, although there seemed to be less spray. My relief was a bit late, and just before he arrived, I heard the now-familiar sound of the Old Man bawling somebody out in the wheelhouse. As I left the bridge, a quick boggle through the window showed that it was all fairly anonymous: somebody somewhere was catching a blast at the other end of a telephone.

On my way aft, I passed through the engineers' accommodation for convenience and safety, and noticed the Third Engineer smiling to himself in the engineers' small pantry, as he made a pot of tea. Putting two and two together, I stopped and asked if everything was alright down below in the engine room.

The Third's smile broadened, and he said that he did not really think so just yet. Apparently the Old Man had a fad about putting 'Engines Labouring' in the deck log book at the end of each watch in really bad weather; the thing was for the Bridge Officer to ask, and for the Engineer Officer to say 'Yes' or 'No'. The answer had been 'Yes' for the last five or six watch-endings. At the end of the last watch, the Third had rung the bridge to give the engine revolutions and sea temperature. The information was accepted, and a voice asked, 'Are the engines labouring?' The Third, thinking it was the Second Mate, answered,

'They were up to about twenty minutes ago, but they then gave birth to a dear little Perkins diesel which looks to be about eight horse-power. They are both doing fine.'

'Oh,' I laughed, 'I heard the Old Man wrapping into someone

over a phone as I left the bridge; you obviously picked the Old Man instead of the Second Mate. What happened?'

'Well,' the Third said, 'the Second Engineer is always sort of half-asleep when he gets down below, so when I realised what had happened I handed the phone to him, told him the Old Man wanted to speak to him, and beat it. When I had climbed to the top of the engine room, I looked down and there was the Second Engineer holding the phone at arm's length, and looking very wide awake indeed. How long can the Old Man swear for?'

'About seven minutes,' I said with feeling.

Next morning, after breakfast, I reported to the Mate who told me to square up around the bridge and chart-room, but to stay out of the Old Man's way as he was getting a bit grizzly through lack of sleep. From the bridge I noted the change in the weather; bright blue sky and a few clouds. The wind did not seem to have dropped at all, but it must have done because there was next to no spray flying about, except that started by the ship's movement in the water, and visibility was good. The swell was long and high; mountainous is a description often seen in print, but hardly ever used at sea, but it would have done so on this occasion. The glass continued to rise.

I spent the morning on the bridge doing odd jobs and the same in the afternoon, until it was time for me to take the second wheel in the twelve-to-four watch. That wheel was quite simple as the ship was riding well. This was good because the Old Man was shown to be very short-tempered and twice tore the Second Mate up for arse paper over some real or imagined fault; nasty it was, people should not really say that sort of thing to other people.

The Mate appeared at four o'clock, just as I had been relieved from the wheel. 'Looks and feels much better,' I heard him say to the Old Man. It still all looked monstrous to me.

About half an hour later my mate came round with a warning

from the bridge that the ship was to turn and run on her old course; this would mean heavy rolling on the turn, and the need to keep a wary eye on the quarter before and during any venture onto the main deck.

We turned, with increased engine noise, and started bucketing off on course again. The motion was unpleasant, but she shipped no heavy water, in spite of large heaps of the stuff continually threatening her stern.

So the Old Man had been as crafty as usual. He had waited for the Mate's opinion on sea and swell, knowing that the Mate had not been on the bridge for about four hours and would therefore notice any change in that time more than he, who had been up there continuously. Also, of course, he had used the last couple of hours of daylight to try the ship back on course.

The NUC balls were being taken down by Chippy's army dodger. Unfortunately they got out of hand just as Chippy arrived on the bridge to see the Mate. The balls fell on Chippy; luckily they were basket, and not the steel collapsible shapes that some ships used.

By the next day a vast improvement in the weather was evident. The swell had dropped away and the ship was rolling only moderately; our speed, while hardly in the ocean-greyhound class, was very good.

'The Liverpool Judies have got her in tow,' remarked Hank. When I asked what he meant, he went on: 'For some reason, about two days out of Liverpool the speed of an inward-bound ship seems to pick up, and seamen reckon that it is the girls in Liverpool who are getting fed up with waiting for them, and have somehow managed to influence matters. Pure imagination, of course, but it only seems to happen for Liverpool and not for any other port.'

The next thing to strike the ship was 'Channels'. With the news of our destination had come what Four Eyes had called the entry into the 'Kiss Me Arse Latitudes' and a general end-of-term feeling arose. With the imminent end of the voyage everybody went very slightly and very safely mad. Not everybody caught it at the same time and someone doing something daft would be explained away by the statement, 'Oh, he's got Channels'.

You did not have to be going up the English Channel to catch 'Channels': they were caught before arrival at any British port from any direction. Passengers are immune from the complaint; only crew members suffer.

The gale over, it was back to the more mundane task of getting the ship as smart as possible for arrival in the UK; hence being given one of the jobs I always disliked most, as I found that I could rarely do it really properly. The rails around the bridge decks were surmounted by untreated teak rails; it was called teak, but it always looked to me to be some sort of Texas Gooseberry Tree wood and I felt the owners had been done when the ship was built. Anyway, the smartening-up of these bare rails was carried out by rubbing them vigorously with a flat wad of canvas, after they had been covered with wet sand. The exact order was phrased, 'Sand and Canvas the Bridge Rails'. The wily Chief Officer had timed one cadet doing the job and wiping the rails clean as he went. The job was finished, but a lot of wet sand splashes appeared on other parts of the bridge structure. The Mate, in his most kind and careful manner, explained the full system.

'I asked you to sand and canvas the rails and we now know how long it takes you, and that is my time. Now, on the way through, you seem to have inadvertently splashed sand all over the bridge bright-work and paint-work; that needs cleaning off, and the cleaning can be done always in your time!'

The only other untreated wood in the ship was the wooden

decks. These were cleaned with salt water and Holy Stones, the latter being a block of sandstone attached to a broom handle by a metal fitting, and these were pushed backward and forwards over sand-sprinkled and wetted decks; not too vigorously though, as there was an awful lot of deck area to cover. The actual block of sandstone was known as a Bible; for use in corners, small tablets of the sandstone were used, on hands and knees, and called Prayer Books.

I found that, providing the Mate was out of the way, a Prayer Book cleaned off the bridge rails much better than his bloody sand and canvas, with no mess left in other directions to clean up afterwards. However, much as he might admire the finished rails, there was always a row if he came up in the middle of the operation and found Prayer Books in evidence.

Asking the Second Officer what difference it made, produced the answer, 'Goodness knows; Bottom Bunk, Top Two Drawers.' This last came from the fact that when, as was usually the case, two-tiered wooden bunks had a set of four wooden drawers underneath, the seaman who occupied the lower berth laid claim to the top two drawers and the upper bunk man had the two lower ones. Nobody knew why and consequently instead of saying, 'It is just one of those things' about a reason for something, the term 'Bottom Bunk, Top Two Drawers' was often employed instead.

Of course, many terms, phrases and customs only applied to a particular shipping company or line and not throughout the entire Merchant Service.

To digress, I feel that the Royal Navy will never truly understand the Merchant Service, as they regard it as an entity. In fact, the set-up could be compared very roughly with the army, with the shipping companies replacing regiments, not having very much to do with each other at all.

With the event of the 'Channels', the Arab firemen started speaking to me again. Not that they got the malady very seriously, they were always slightly apart from the rest of the crew, their behaviour being impeccable at all times, and of course they had never taken a drink when the rest of the crowd had, it being against their religion. Anyway, they had stopped speaking to me after an occurrence during one of the four-to-eight morning watches in the tropics.

I was stand-by man with the job of calling certain members of the crew at differing times. The lookout man had been knocked off and I had just seen him aft getting a cup of tea; in fact I could place everybody in the ship.

Suddenly there was the most almighty scream from the region of the engine room, plainly heard because our dear old steam engines were almost silent. I started running for the engine room door and had nearly reached it when out stumbled the fireman on watch in the boiler room and collapsed moaning on the deck; what a mess he was in! Covered in blood and a greyish, whitish goo, chiefly around the head. Footsteps pounding up the ladders heralded the arrival of the Second Engineer Officer and the other Arab fireman of the watch, who had been acting as greaser in the engine room.

The Second shouted to me to get the Chief Steward and tell him it looked like a serious head injury. I needed no second bidding; I had fairly recently seen a school acquaintance's body after he'd been run over by a bus and the brains oozing about had looked rather similar to this lot.

The Chief Steward dived out of his bunk, grabbed his handily-kept first aid satchel and went to the gently moaning fireman. Whistling out his breath, he began to clean around the man's head to ascertain the actual extent of the wound. He cleaned further and further without finding the injury, and then began to swear in a rather puzzled way. I left to get on with my own job, as there were now plenty of assistants and I had become surplus to requirements. Later I was sent for by the Old Man and from the looks I received on the way there I felt there was trouble of some kind brewing; it must have something to do with the accident, as nothing else had happened for days.

When I reached his cabin, the Old Man was looking very unenthralled. 'Did you see any flying fish lying on the deck this morning at daybreak?' he snarled.

'Yes, Sir,' I replied, 'there was a particularly large one by number three hatch. The reason that I did not throw it overboard was because it was so large and I thought people would be interested to see such a beauty.'

'Well, Old Yussef was taking a breather from his boilers and was sitting under one of the boiler room ventilators fitted with a down-draught fan. Somebody chucked that flying fish down the vent. The old boy was suddenly hit by a mass of chopped up blood and guts, and quite naturally panicked, thinking he had been injured somehow. Was it you?'

'No, Sir,' I answered.

'Get out!' he snarled.

It was not me and I knew that nobody else was about. That left one person. The bloody Mate must have nipped down from the bridge and done the deed: it just fitted his sense of humour. I was more certain of his guilt when he never mentioned the affair to me.

The evening deck meetings continued, with the Chief Engineer an informal and background chairman.

'What is the Pool that everybody seems to talk about belonging to?' I asked one evening

The answer came. 'Before the war, if you wanted a job in a

ship you had to walk around the company offices and around the ships themselves until you found a vacancy; and before the war you often had to walk a bloody long way for a bloody long time! Come the war, a central office was set up in each port, liaising with other ports, and so a sort of nautical Labour Exchange was formed. Very handy system: a ship applied directly to the local office for seamen, and seamen went direct to the same place for jobs, simple. Nowadays it's called the Shipping Federation, but the lay term is the Pool. You can be on contract to the Pool, in which case they pay you if there is no job, or you can just register there and use it casually. It's a pretty good system; I think the shipowners pay a levy for each man they take from the Pool and that's what keeps it going. It does not seem to be a government job, or, if it is, it does not show because they are too efficient.'

You could find out by listening to the chat how life went on ashore at Sunday lunch times, for example. Pubs all over England closed at two o'clock. Seamen all over England left the pubs at quarter past two. Seamen's wives all over England put Sunday lunch on the table at one o'clock. This time gap meant that a man went home for a dish that had been in the oven for an hour and a half or so; there was nearly always a row.

'I think,' said the first, 'that if you go in, eat it and say it's nice, they just smoulder all afternoon and then explode about something else in the evening.'

'Yes,' said the second, 'it's much, much better to go in, eat it and say it's horrible and get the noise over straight away.'

'The other way,' said a third, 'is to go in and say you are not hungry at all, this takes the wind out of their sails, but there is a delayed bang; usually about Tuesday or Wednesday.'

Deaf Charlie said, with the air of a connoisseur in such matters, 'What I tried once was to go in, start eating it and then say how nice it was, so what mistake had she made? The resulting noise and fireworks were up to expectation, but she spoiled it by hitting me with an aluminium colander; so hard in fact that I had to buy her a new one. I should have stuck to iron gear – Elastoplast is cheaper than colanders.'

Another time the Chief Engineer was queried about nautical novels.

'Say, Chief, we always read in books about ships being scuttled or sunk by opening the sea-cocks. Have we got any sea-cocks?'

'No,' said the Chief emphatically, 'no British ship has. Ships are designed and thought out by naval architects, the Board of Trade, the owners and the shipbuilders, with the sole idea of keeping water out of the vessel. The last thing anybody wants is a valve that lets water directly into the bloody thing; sure as shit some hunk head would open it to see what happened. No, to scuttle a ship needs a little bit of time and ingenuity coupled with a fair amount of spanner work. To disable a ship is much more simple. Here you would just need to dump the Old Man's typewriter, the Mate's tape-measure and the chart-room rubber over the site, stamp on Four Eyes' glasses and the whole job would shudder to an irreparable halt in no time.'

Derivations of terms and customs was also a subject that came up frequently. Any question could be chucked in and an answer received; somebody would have read or heard an answer somewhere.

'Why do they call a square structure in the middle of a ship the bridge?'

'That comes from the days of the early paddle steamers. The boxes covering the paddle wheels on each side of the ship stood well above the main deck and hid the view from aft; they were also found to be the best vantage points nearest the engines. It was found inconvenient to rush down from the top of one, across the main deck and up the other. Somebody put a walkway, gangway or bridge between the top of the two; it was the name "bridge" that stuck.'

Noah's Ark came up for discussion one evening, not so much on the religious aspect, but more on the practical. It appeared that Sir Isaac Newton, in his off-watch time and between falling apples, had worked out the length of a cubit. One of the things he practised the result on was the Ark. The result he obtained was 10,000 tons.

He obviously meant measurement tons rather than displacement, or actual tons weight; but with a measurement ton being 100 cubic feet, she must still have been quite a large barge.

At this point three from the group broke away to get to work with Bibles and log tables with the idea of working backwards to find out how long a cubit was. I forget the three different answers they came back with. As the Chief remarked, there was nothing we needed to know more!

We were heading through the bay for a point off the Scilly Isles. Coming on the wheel for the middle watch, I found she was steering well and needed little help. The Second Mate seemed to be keeping his watch on the wheelhouse/chartroom deck, and not on the Monkey Island, which was more usual when we were clear of the land. He was diving into the chartroom about every quarter of an hour, and I could hear him running the echo sounding machine for a minute or so each time.

Why? I knew we were in deep water. He seemed in a good mood, so I asked him.

'Oh, we're coming up to the 100 fathom line, and as that line is marked on the chart it will give a position line I can put the time and log reading beside.' He had a look round outside. 'I'll take the wheel; go and have a quick look at the chart.'

The chart showed a very shallow rise both before and after the line, and I mentioned this when I returned.

'Yes,' he said, 'but in this game you grab any information you can.'

About half an hour later he announced that we had crossed the much-vaunted line, and stomped up to the Monkey Island. We could both get some peace and bloody quiet now.

Next morning we were on the 'English Channel and Western Approaches' chart; the course took us twelve miles off Round Island lighthouse in the western Scillies.

The watch system my mate and myself had was rather handy; he the four to eight and me the twelve to four. One of us about the bridge for sixteen hours a day and in the eight to twelve forenoon watch one of us was often up there on odd jobs anyway.

There began to be more shipping about, either on crossing courses or the opposite one to us. I remarked to the Second Mate that as the approaching ships had probably used Round Island lighthouse as a departure point from St George's Channel we must be on the right course.

'Bollocks!' he said. 'You should never draw conclusions from the courses of other craft; remember the man that followed the Thames barge that was going to load sand.'

I decided to keep quiet for the rest of my wheel.

When not on the wheel during the day, I was working on deck with Deaf Charlie, Jan, and often Hank. When a ship passed close enough to recognise, one of them would usually comment on the owning company; one of the others would usually come out with something derogatory about the owners or the running of them.

'One of Counties Ship Management "Hill" boats.'

'Hilly Billy would be a better name.'

One with a white funnel band and red triangle in it.

'Lambert Brothers' Temple boat.'

'Bass boat, pity they don't carry much on board.'

Black funnel, white band with a red band in the middle of it.

128

'Harrisons of Liverpool.'

'Yeah. Two of fat and one of lean.'

'Shaw Savill and Albion.'

'Sure Starvation and Agony.'

'Hogarth, Baron boat.'

'Hungry Hogarth, barren boat.'

A stately P & O freighter.

'Bloody left-handed gentlemen.'

I was going to enquire about this last, when a handwhistle blast from the bridge sent me up there to find what the bloody hell they wanted up there now!

The log was foul; watch to clear it.

The Patent Log was a device for telling the distance through the water the vessel had run. There was a brass tube with offset vanes called the Rotator which was towed behind the ship on about 200 ft of braided line connected to a clock on board. The rotator turned the line and wound the clock round to show one mile about every six minutes for ten knots. In a watch it turned about 40 miles.

The accuracy depended on the length of line; shorten the line to increase the reading, lengthen it to decrease. There was a governor wheel between the end of the log line and the clock. The line was disconnected from the governor and then we pulled in like mad. It had to be quick, as the rotator was still rotating and putting turns into the log line. Once there was enough in for one man to handle the rest, the other two started letting the end of the line out from the opposite quarter so the twists would take themselves out. Then heave it all in again, and flake it up and down the deck ready for streaming again. Never did know what had fouled the line on the rotator, as it must have fallen clear when disturbed.

Back to working on deck. Jan was a good worker, but the

faster he worked, the more he talked, usually about ships he had been on. We couldn't understand much of it, but one bit made me drop my brush laughing. '. . . Yah, she was a bad ship, but that was the straw which broke the turkey's quack.'

I was on the wheel for the last two hours; the Old Man and Sparkie were up there using the direction finding machine. Round Island has a radio beacon and they were, together with the Second Officer, trying to get a bearing, but we were still a fair way off.

My mate was a bit late relieving me, very unusual. As we were handing over to each other the Old Man said to the Second, 'Take the wheel for a little, I want to show the two lads the chart.' He had a smile on his face; he must have caught the 'Channels' we thought.

The 'Western Approaches to the Channel' chart was open on the table.

'Ever heard the song "Spanish Ladies?"' he asked. We nodded. 'Well, there is one verse that goes:

'We hove the ship to with the wind at SW boys,
We hove our ship to, to strike soundings clear,
We got 45 fathoms, and a clear sandy bottom;
We filled our main topsail up channel to steer.

'Well, the chap that wrote that knew his navigation; it is a small lesson in itself. Here, on this large chart, is the only small area that has a fine sand bottom in 45 fathoms and if you filled your topsail you'd be heading NE, that is, straight up the middle of the Channel.'

To my mate, 'You'd better get back on the wheel, the Second Officer isn't much good at it; he used to try and write his name in the ship's wake when he was a cadet!'

I talked to the Third Mate about the chances of leave.

'Ah! said the Third, 'don't push your luck. Don't pack or pull out best gear, or show any signs of expecting to go. If some stupid sod asks you about going on leave in the Mate's hearing just go pie-faced and say that you expect that will depend on what work is needed aboard ship, and that there is almost bound to be too much once the crew has been paid off.'

I met Sparks on deck before tea; he was a bit upset, poor old bugger. 'It's always the same with D.F. bearings,' he said. 'You spend all trip passing D.F. stations and asking the Watch Officer to assist in calibrating the set, but it is never convenient for them. Yet the day we start crossing a large stretch of tidal stream, such as the English Channel, they jump on you to give them accurate bearings. You watch, they'll get past Round Island and heading up to the Smalls and the whole performance will start again.'

When I was next on the bridge it was still fine and clear; Jan handed the wheel over to me. 'I think we take this weather right up to the "pool".' He qualified this. 'Mine arse itches!'

The Second was in and out of the wheelhouse, very cheery and quite chatty. We'd passed Round Island about right and with the tidal stream going in and out of the Bristol Channel in equal proportions we should do well making the Smalls.

The Smalls was passed with a lot of talk about Doubling the Angle On the Bow and Four Point Bearings. These mystical things, when looked up, turned out to be two quite simple geometrical position-finding ploys using two bearings taken off the same terrestrial object with an interval between. Providing there was no effect by wind or current the distance-off at the second bearing was the same as was steamed between the two bearings. How far had we steamed between the two bearings? Was it log distance? Was it the 'give a speed of ten knots' that the Old Man suggested? Oh well! Navigation Is Not An Exact Science, someone once said.

131

Looking it up was consulting a large tome named *Nicholl's Concise Guide*, Volume One; if concise meant short, I fervently hoped I never came across the full bloody volume! Later I found it was a very handy volume which became very battered with usage. Later still I discovered there was a Volume Two . . .

An army dodger standing on the deck, wearing a surprised expression.

'What's up?' I grunted as I passed.

'Hank's spoken to me for the second day running without swearing at me!' he said.

'What did he say?' I asked.

He said,

> 'You yellow looking,
> Tallow looking,
> Tin-faced, juicy-eyed,
> Son of an hangman's ghost,
> Dabbled in blood.'

Quite descriptive; I said, 'What did he say yesterday?'

'He called me a Pissbegotten, Ply-faced Punk,' was the answer.

The loom of Bardsey Island light appeared, then the light itself. The Second Officer naturally took a bearing as soon as the light itself showed; coming out of the chartroom he said he had used it for a Dipping Bearing. He explained that when a lighthouse first showed you could get a distance from it by going into Nories Tables with the charted height of the light as one figure and your own height of eye from the sea as the second figure; the table gave a distance away; he said it was not necessarily too accurate in tidal waters. She was apparently going at a very good speed; we would be rounding Anglesey and into Liverpool Bay during the next watch.

Eight o'clock next morning we had rounded Anglesey; and Four Eyes pointed to the land.

'That's Molfre in there; very nasty shipwreck there in the late eighteen-fifties. Well-found ship called the *Royal Charter*, good-sized crew and officers and a load of passengers. She'd had trouble with a storm in the Irish Sea, but had got round here out of it.

'The storm suddenly came in from the N.E. at hurricane force and in spite of everything the Old Man did she was driven onto the jagged rocks that abound just here. They got a line ashore, but the thirty or so villagers that came to help were farmers and obviously did not know what to do with it. So the Master sent some seamen ashore and a form of breeches buoy was soon set up. There was a squawk afterwards because some bloody journalist tried to claim that crew had landed before women and children, but that happens all too often. The ship was breaking up fast, and much valuable time was wasted by the women refusing to go because they were frightened; the men were naturally reluctant to go before the females. So it ended up sadly with very few people getting off at all.

'The local people had been as helpful as possible; some being injured helping survivors out of the rock-studded shore, and giving what meagre shelter they could in their cottages. The *Royal Charter* was carrying gold among her cargo and this broke out of its boxes and was scattered over the rocks. Obviously not all of it was recovered; I expect a bit of it remained hidden in the area until the heat was off. It's not at all infrequent for people who risk their necks helping save life to have no scruples about secreting inanimate stuff for their own benefit.'

I'd never heard Four Eyes speak in such an interesting fashion and thought it was probably his way of manifesting 'the Channels'.

After breakfast the Mate sent for us.

'I have a nice little job for you,' he beamed. Oh, bloody hell;

what this time?

'You'll note the sailors have white-leaded and tallowed all the stays in the ship except the bottom half of the funnel stays, which can be reached from the decks. Now you go and finish the bottom half; it looks a messy job, but you'll find the white lead and tallow will clean your hands up well. Come and see me when you have finished.'

We put the gunge on with a wad of cotton waste and our hands. He was right as usual. It did clean our hands. We went to him an hour or so later.

He looked up from his deck. 'Hands OK? Good. Now take these old cotton gloves and wear them till we're in and tied up.'

Glory be! The Mate giving gear away. Must be his 'Channels' manifesting themselves.

My mate said, 'In and tied up, Sir? Are we not waiting at the Bar light vessel?' This was apparently often the usual thing for ships with bulk cargoes.

'Yes, we are locking in at 1600. The Master had a telegram twenty minutes ago,' the Mate said blandly.

Dear me! The Old Man giving secret information away as soon as he got it! Must have 'Channels' too!

'Yes,' the Mate said, seeing we had digested the information, 'you fellows dodge around and help where you can; the more we can do now, the sooner everybody can get on the piss after we're tied up.' He sat back, clasped his hands, and looked at the deckhead. 'The last does not include you, of course.'

We weren't allowed on the wheel in close traffic; so spent the time giving the odd hand in the odd place, but never together; single cadets, we had learned, are not a unit to be sent off to do something tangible. I helped Chippy a bit with his wedges, and then Four Eyes for a bit getting guys spread and derricks ready to top. The weather was still superb, Jan's itching arse had told the truth.

I then spied the old Chief Engineer sitting on a hatch in a warm place, making sennit out of condenser cord, so I went and gave him a hand; the Mate had said anyone. He was making a square sennit using eight strands of cords. He'd showed me how to earlier in the voyage, and at the time I'd thought it strange to learn a type of knotting from an Engineer. He had explained that sennit was a kind of plaiting; it could be round, triangular, flat, or the square type he liked to make for packing steam glands.

He went and got his big pipe while I did a bit of sennit; then started smoking it. The system was that I did a bit while he had a smoke, then he did a bit while I had a smoke. It did not take me long to realise that his pipe took far longer to fill and smoke than it did for me to just smoke a cigarette; the head-working old bastard.

A Clan boat came past; black funnel with two red bands.

The Chief chuckled. 'Did you hear about the two Clan line cadets who at the ending of a trip were told to paint their cabin out? Yeh, well they thought that the pale cream was a bit dull, so they mixed just a hint of blue into the paint.

'The Old Man and Chief Officer were having an end-of-voyage look around the ship and entered the cadets' cabin; the cadets were sent for, and told they did not go home until the cabin was painted properly in company colours. It had been a long trip and everybody two-blocks with it, not least the cadets.

'The next day, long after most people had gone on leave, the Old Man saw the cadets going down the gangway with all their gear; he rushed down to the Chief Officer, and they both made a dive for the cadets' cabin.

'It was painted in Company colours. Pure black throughout, with two red bands around the bulkhead.'

The Chief chatted on. 'On a normal working day, what's the

difference between a Deck Officer and an Engineer Officer?'

I said I didn't know.

'The Deck Officer washes his hands after he goes to the lavatory, the Engineer Officer before.'

The Third Officer came past and stopped when he saw me.

'I've been looking for one of you two,' he said, looking over his shoulder. 'Don't start packing to go on leave yet, wait until we are in, tied up and signed off; then go along to the Mate in your working gear, and ask if there is any chance of going on leave. He'll look very doubtful, run through your faults for the voyage, looking even more doubtful, and then say yes. I know, I played that game with him several times; he's not a bad old bastard, really.'

I told my mate later and his response was typical. 'Of course the devious sod will send us home; fits in with him going to the trouble of keeping a job for the last day that would clean our hands up!'

The Chief and I kept on senniting away; with the pile on deck and what was secreted in his cabin already we must have made several nautical miles during the trip. (6080 ft as to 5280 ft.) Enough to outfit the ship for 30 years anyway.

Hank came past and stopped. 'The Mate has just asked me back next trip, she's going out light to the West Coast. Suits me. I want a short trip to fit my sister's wedding in.'

'West Coast of Africa,' muttered the Chief, 'shorter sea trips in and out of odd ports while we're down there. Yes, the long sea trips of this voyage are not really much use to you cadets. Tell me, if you kept a diary, what would you have put in it to cover the last five weeks, apart from that bad weather?'

The old bugger was too near the truth, because I did and there wasn't!

'Um,' ruminated the Chief, 'going down the West Coast means

bunkering at Las Palmas; I think I have a little business to conduct with the Old Rope Man there.'

I thought no more of the remark until next trip, when I saw him conducting several sacks down the gangway in the dusk. The last had a short length of all too familiar sennit sticking out of it!

A ship of the Bank line passed outward bound; buff funnel with a black top, house flag in red and blue diagonally divided with a white stripe crossing both on the opposite diagonal.

'Huh,' says Hank. Usual derogatory remarks coming, I thought. 'The red of blood and the blue of cold crossed by the bone of contention.' What would they think of next? I'd met at home a Bank line officer and he was quite happy with them, except that they tended to go away for two years or more at a time, which apparently you got used to.

Hank looked forward, turned away, then looked sharply back. 'Prince boat,' he said over his shoulder.

'What's a Prince boat?' I said to the Chief idly as we sat on the hatch continuing to sennit.

'The Prince Line Limited, started on the Tyne by Jimmy Knott, or Sir James Knott, as he became; started with nothing, then bought odd shares in odd ships until he became an owner. They have a round-the-world service; also a Mediterranean line operating from London or Manchester. One of their ships, the *Belgian Prince*, was the first commercial ship up the Great, Grey, Green, Greasy Manchester Ship Canal, and they've been running out of there ever since. It's widely assumed by seamen that he had a small share in building it; a very shrewd and astute man. He always expected a lot of work out of his people, but for his time he treated them much better than a lot of other outfits.

'Rumour has it that King Edward VII, when he was Prince of Wales, got on the bottle with Jimmy Knott and the outcome was that he told Jimmy he could wear the Prince of Wales' Feathers on his funnels; Jimmy responded by renaming his company The Prince Line. True or false, they are the only British company to have a Royal emblem on their funnels, others weakly point out that they have them on their House flags, but so do the Prince boats.'

Hank came and sat on the hatch beside us as the ship in question came into view. She was very smart, but not a usual sort of shape. I remarked that by her bow wave she was going only half ahead.

Hank laughed. 'That speed you see is flat out; I know, I spent about four bloody months on her; it would only have been two if she had a decent size engine. She lifts about 9,500 tons of cargo, so she's quite a lump to push round the ocean; she has the smallest Doxford diesel I've ever seen, outside a model shop, and of all things it's only a three cylinder one.'

She was a strange ship from the start. She was built by a yard that closed down during the slump except for the various yard apprentices; when they found the time hanging heavily on the lads' hands, some bright bastard said, 'Let's build a ship out of the spare pieces we have lying round the yard.' They made a list of all the pieces, sent it to a naval architect, and he designed what was to become the *African Prince*! She was finished about 1937; some of her steam winches had plates on them reading "Reconditioned 1911"! It paid off during the war though; every torpedo that was fired at her passed at least half a mile ahead as no U-Boat commander dreamt a ship could go that slow.

'Somehow I enjoyed my time in her. The food was good, the overtime was terrific; the Company wanted its cargoes carried and landed in first-class condition. They also wanted their ships in first-class condition. They didn't mind if we drank a hell of a lot of beer when we weren't working, and always made sure there was plenty on board.' Hank laughed and went on his way.

Strange! Nobody had said anything scurrilous about the company!

The telegraphs jangled, must be Stand By Engines for the Pilot; the trip had started to end. I thought I would gently mosey along and have a look if I could help with the pilot ladder. It was time to move off the hatch anyway; Chippy was moving round it knocking out wedges with his maul and his favourite army dodger was following him up closely bagging them.

Suddenly there was a sort of 'humph' sound and the army dodger collapsed on the deck; Chippy was withdrawing the handle end of his maul from the place his stomach had been.

'That'll teach the rude little bastard,' Chippy muttered.

'What's up, Chippy,' I asked.

'What's up?' flashed Chippy. 'That tuppenny-halfpenny sod is. I've been called and referred to as a hell of a lot of things, but that was the bloody limit. Halfway through the lunch break the Bo'sun detailed him to gather wedges for me this afternoon. When he did not go with the rest of the crowd they asked him why. He turned to his mates and says, "I've got to go with old Chuckle pants." He didn't know I heard, and I've been waiting the whole afternoon for him to get near enough to fix. Chuckle pants, indeed!'

I continued towards the pilot ladder which I could hear going overside; I noted there was no heaving line for the pilot's bag, so I went and got one. The pilot cutter edged in towards us, and then dropped a boat with the pilot aboard which came alongside. It was crewed by two lads not much older than myself.

'Apprentices,' someone said. 'They do four years of that then they can go for their Second Mate's exam.'

I thought it looked an easy way of getting time in; but I changed my view radically when at a later date I saw them working in a near gale!

I carried the pilot's bag up to the bridge with him following me. I thought I'd do a bit of tidying up around it. With leave in mind I wanted to be seen to be keen. Creeping? Too bloody right!

The pilot was an elderly man and knew the score; about the first thing he said to the Old Man, after the introductions had been made, was: 'You can top the derricks if you want. They won't be in my way in weather like this. It's not often you can see the Liver Building from here at this time of year; it will save time after you dock and the lads will get up the road for a beer sooner.'

I decided to stay on the bridge until the derricks were up. Once they were, I decided to go forr'd and polish the ships's bell; anybody that was interested would see me beavering away. Chippy was on the fo'c's'le and had been there since the bar, ready to let go an anchor if needed. He watched me polishing the bell.

'What's the nicest use a merchant ship's bell is ever put to, and that does not include ringing it?' he asked very casually.

Half expecting a trap, I answered equally casually, 'I don't know, Chippy.'

'Well,' he said quietly, 'on the very, very rare occasion that there is a baby christened aboard a merchant vessel, the ship's bell is removed from the fo'c's'le, taken to the place of the ceremony inverted and used as a font. I always find that rather nice. Mind you, if you are on a ship where you know the bell has been used for that purpose it can make you think a bit. A windy night, with cold horizontal rain blowing across the fo'c's'le, working two anchors and their cables, with something going wrong, the language between fo'c's'le and bridge can be appalling. I often wonder as I ring the anchor shackles up and down, if the baby's ears are burning somewhere!'

That was another use for the ship's bell: when the anchors were being used. Anchor cables have a shackle every fifteen fathoms of their length, and it is customary to talk of any measurement of cable by the term 'shackle'. If I remember correctly, that first ship had ten shackles of cable on one anchor and twelve shackles on the other, that is 900 feet and 12080 feet of chain cable respectively. Rarely was the whole amount of chain cable used: it depended on the depth of water, or the berth the ship was going to. Anyway, as the first shackle went overboard Chippy rang one stroke on the bell, and with the second, two strokes, and so on. Weighing the anchor meant that the number of bells were sounded in reverse; with the anchor leaving the bottom on being 'aweigh' a continuous ringing of the bell for about five seconds signalled that fact to the bridge.

At anchor in fog, the bell was used as a fog signal and was meant to be rung continuously for five seconds about every minute, followed by a gong sounded aft for another five seconds. The evolution was doomed mostly to fifty percent failure; the bell was bolted securely forward, but the gong unhappily was portable and nobody could ever find the bloody thing. However, this was a time when it paid to have kept in with the Chief Cook, because with the least of cajolery he would lend his largest iron frying pan and that was hung up and beaten with a well clothed wooden stick. The gong was never lost, you just never could find it when you wanted it. It would turn up later as the tray in the bottom of somebody's parrot cage, or someone like Hank would be attempting to grow tulip bulbs in it.

Deaf Charlie approached the fo'c's'le and relieved Chippy to go for a mug of tea. A minute later Hank turned up and relieved Deaf Charlie who made off looking disgruntled. I asked Hank what was the matter and he smilingly explained.

'This company is very old-fashioned, and they remember an old tale; consequently they will not have anybody deaf on their fo'c's'le heads during standby.' He went on to tell me the old tale.

A ship was ending her voyage with a Chippy and a Mate, who was a bit deaf, standing by on the fo'c's'le. Chippy and Mate had been at loggerheads the whole voyage.

'Chippy,' said the Mate. 'As soon as we get in, you can catch the first train home. I've never had such an useless, lazy bugger as a Chippy in all my time as Mate. I don't want you waiting for a relief or ever to set eyes on you again once we get in; so remember you are to catch the first train home.'

The ship went on slowly up river and then the Old Man shouted forward, 'We are going port-side to in the lock.'

'Port what was that, Chippy?' asked the deaf Mate.

'Let go port anchor,' said the stony-faced Chippy.

'All right, let go port anchor,' ordered the Mate.

Amidst the diminishing thunder of the cable running, the Old Man was heard to be going berserk on his bridge.

'What's he saying now, Chippy?' shouted the Mate.

'Let go starboard anchor, Sir,' said Chippy, still stony-faced.

'All right, let go starboard anchor,' ordered the Mate.

When the ship was brought up by about four shackles of each cable leading astern, silence reigned, until broken by the semi-speechless Old Man from the bridge, yelling disjointedly.

'What's he saying now, Chippy?' asked the Mate.

'He is saying,' said Chippy enthusiastically, 'that you are catching the same train home that I am!'

I finished polishing the bell, collected my cleaning gear, and made my way aft chuckling, to return to the bridge. The Old Man had disappeared to do some paperwork, and the Second Mate and the pilot took to passing the time of day.

'Is the old tale true that the two bronze birds on the Liver Building flap their wings every time a woman of untarnished virtue passes?' asked the Second innocently.

'Not since the air raids when their wings were trimmed off in case of blast,' said the pilot very seriously.

'What is a Liver Bird anyway; are they birds of fantasy?'

'Not at all. There was a pool where Liverpool now stands and a fairly rare weed with a Latin name grew in it. Some birds called Liver birds flourished in the pool and it became known as the Liverpool; the birds had a Latin name too.

'It originally had a Welsh name, something like Lwpl; the Welsh never put any vowels in their words and the Romans never seemed to know their V from their W, according to our Latin masters. So, all in all that would seem to be some time ago.

'Industry sprang up on the Mersey, the weed in the pool died and the birds flew away, whether to extinction or not I don't know.'

We went on up the river with the pilot chatting away. The pilot must have sensed Deaf Charlie's affliction, because he always spoke full face to him and gave hand instructions.

'There are our tugs, Captain,' to the Old Man, who had reappeared.

'Stand by Forr'd and Aft,' the Old Man ordered the First and Second Officers.

I went aft and got the warping winch turning over quietly after some banging as the water in the line went through the cylinders. The after tug came alongside on the quarter and gave us his line. I thought that would be easier than giving them ours, but it turned out to be harder, as it was thick wire and we had to get over half of it in before the tug skipper told us to turn it up on the bitts.

So we edged into the lock; there was no wind so the steam from the winch was around like a thick bank of fog. I assumed that somebody somewhere who could see what was going on would occasionally tell us what was required.

Driving the warping winch was about the safest place to be,

but shouted requests sometimes conflicted; one side would shout 'slack away' at the same time the other shouted 'heave'. Oh, well . . .

Orders were given to make fast stern line and after back spring, so I assumed we were alongside. After waiting a minute or two, I got off the winch and went to talk to Hank leaning over the rail. Ever teaching, he asked me if I had noted how the pilot told the tugs what he wanted, and I said I had not.

'The pilot blows the ship's whistle to the after tug and a hand whistle to the forr'd tug.'

'What's a hand whistle?' I said.

'One he holds in his hand and blows with his mouth; or I suppose he could stuff it up his arse and fart, it would have the same effect, but he would still hold it in his hand,' he said disgustedly.

'By the way, Hank, when you and the Chief were talking about that ship called the *African Prince* neither of you said anything derogatory about her or the company; unusual, wasn't it?'

Hank looked thoughtful. 'Yeah, I suppose so, come to think of it I only heard one guy get clever and ask why she had a lavatory brush on her funnel? The regular crew jumped on him and threw him over the rail. Don't look startled. We were in port and he was an uninvited visitor. Only thing was that he couldn't swim; luckily there was a heaving line handy which someone tied a running noose on and the first shoot went round one arm and his neck.

'They hauled him onto the quay, careful, mind you, so as not to break his arm; they kicked him in the guts a couple of times to get the water out and brought the heaving line back aboard. Funny, he never came aboard again!'

The next thing that occurred was that out of the steam-laden dusk three or four figures appeared. Definitely Scouse by their voices, as they greeted Hank and Jan by name. They turned out of be taxi drivers who worked the ships; they wanted to know not if, but when various people wanted to go up to various stations, or straight home if they lived locally. They were a mine of odd bits of information.

'The ship's paying off eleven tomorrow morning . . .'

'We've just helped the Old Man's wife aboard, she works out most of the pay-offs for him, together with all the Mickey Mouse forms that go with it; so she'll be up most of the night. She used to work for an accountant; some said that's why he married her . . .'

'They're taking your Christmas Tree off this voyage and putting your old top-masts back up. The Ministry swapped them at the beginning of the war. A survey six months back showed the Tree was rotten and as the top-masts have been lying about on the dock in Liverpool since the war and it'll be cheaper to fix them back than renew the Tree, the Bo'sun will swear because . . .'

'Small party tomorrow, the Zeebrugge Association; they want to go across to Birkenhead on the *Iris*, have lunch, and back on the *Daffodil*, then back up for the London train. They haven't been on them since the St George's Day raid in 1918; they'll probably all get pissed at lunchtime and I'll have to carry 'em on and off the *Daffodil*. Still, there's one thing about the Navy; they won't spew all over my taxi . . .'

Someone on the quay called that the lock gates were opening forr'd, the taxi drivers, except one who stayed to chat, leapt for the dock; we were told to let go and the ship glided into the Dock System. Then it was gently through narrows and across the bottom end of docks, until at last we turned and headed up one. We went nearly to the head of the dock and tied up alongside. It was the fastest and most secure tie-up I had yet witnessed, helped by a willing hand from the remaining taxi-driver who had obviously been a seaman.

Some yelps on the whistle and the tug was let go; The Second Officer called, 'Gangway, lads,' and as we trooped forward there was a frantic jangling of the engine room and bridge telegraphs which went on for longer than was usual.

'Finish with Engines,' said one.

'And so endeth the mighty voyage,' said a second.

'Bloody good job too!' said a third.

The gangway was rigged and lowered into the gathering dusk and various figures detached themselves from the shadows of warehouses to walk slowly toward the bottom of it. Officialdom was arriving.

Hank muttered who they were to me as they passed the foot. 'One Customs Waterguard Officer, there will be two tomorrow to take money on dutiable goods, once we have money from the pay-off; maybe bring the Black Gang (as they call themselves) to rummage the ship if tonight's guy doesn't like the look of something.'

'Port Health Officer, to make sure we don't need quarantine.'

'Ship Chandler, for the Chief Steward. He always likes to be on the spot early.'

'Outside Manager, and Clerk, from the agents.'

'Ours is still in use,' Hank said to one visitor; then to me, 'That's the Old Rope Man.'

To an old man who shuffled aboard, 'Hello, George.' To me, 'That's the nightwatchman. He's been on every ship I've been on in Liverpool, no matter what company.'

'Hello, Jim.' To me, 'That's the night shore donkeyman; he's been on every other bloody ship I've been on in Liverpool!'

'Right-oh lads. That's it, thank you very much,' shouted Four Eyes.

Four Eyes saying 'Thank you' to the crowd! They must have

been his last official words of the trip.

Went and cleaned up; then fiddled about getting ready for a hurried pack the next day but not leaving anything in sight in case the Mate looked in. The people noises of the ship diminished until suddenly we noticed there were none at all. We thought of going ashore and trying to get a beer, but dockside pubs were notoriously strict on under-age drinking. In fact they were notoriously strict about almost everything; understandably, I suppose.

There was a foot on the steel ladder leading onto our deck, and the Third Officer appeared. 'Come and have a beer,' he said, and just avoided getting trampled in the rush.

We went to his cabin, where the Fourth Engineer was already sitting. To our delight 'a beer' turned out to be a pint bottle each; we asked him what the score was as far as the top brass went.

'Oh, the Old Man intimated that as the only people on board this evening would be himself, the Mate and the four of us here, it might be a good idea if I got hold of some beer and the four of us had a drink; there's three bottles each,' the Third Mate said. He paused to drink, and went on to tell us exactly what the Old Man had said.

'If those two brassbound little bastards don't have a drink on board they'll go up the road and get as pissed as handcarts!'

'I asked the remaining taxi driver to nip up the road and he did so gladly,' smiled the Third.

'Yes,' said the Fourth, 'I've always found the dock taxi drivers extremely helpful; I wonder sometimes if they are some sort of descendant of the old Boarding House keepers who looked after seamen; they were always pretty helpful, even if one or two of them did stretch things a bit, such as Paddy West.'

'Who was he?' we asked.

'Huh! Seaboots you do not need, carpet slippers you must

have; he was a Keeper that specialised in finding men who had come to the big city to see the sights, had been rolled, so couldn't go home, and had nowhere to go. He'd take them in, give 'em very rudimentary training, and ship 'em out. Rudimentary, huh! For stoke-hold training he had a barrel, with the ends out, hung up in his backyard; he also had a ton of coal. The embryo stoker was required to sling the coal through the barrel to the other side of the yard; this emulated either a boiler door or a trimming hole.

'In the advanced stage of training the barrel could be set swinging, to simulate the rolling of the ship. Other simulations included Mrs West throwing the odd bucket of water over them from a first floor window (this was obviously water coming down a ventilator) or Paddy touching their arses up with a hot poker (this obviously meant they'd stepped back and come into contact with a hot boiler).

'Deckhand training was more varied; front and back door steps became gangway and brow; cupboards became lockers; stairs became ladders; rooms had decks, deckheads and bulkheads; the shithouse, believe it or not, remained the shithouse.'

One typical seamanship exercise was recorded in verse.

> Paddy sent me to the attic,
> The Main-Royal for to stow,
> And as I climbed the attic ladder,
> My word, the wind did blow;
> But when I reached the attic,
> No Main-Royal could I find,
> So I took a tumble to myself,
> And stowed the window blind.

We then heard that for Chippy the voyage had ended in a particularly happy fashion. While entering the locks a heaving line had been thrown from ashore with a weighted monkey's fist tied in its tail. Chippy's unfortunate army dodger had not been concentrating on the job and received the knot hard on the top of his head, which almost knocked him senseless.

Four Eyes said quietly to Chippy, 'Do you think he has suffered any brain damage?'

Chippy replied bitterly, 'Don't worry, it would be impossible to tell in the case of a dopey bastard like that. He gives my arse earache.'

The talk continued about this, that and bugger all, until a voice called from the other side of the accommodation, 'Third Mate, have you got the cadets there?'

'Yes,' called the Third Mate, and as very slow steps came along the cross-alleyway, he said, 'Quick, hide your beer. He knows, but make it look good.'

The Chief Officer appeared, gloves and torch in hand. 'Evening,' he said, as we stood up. 'I've just been looking around the ship and she's alright except for one thing. There's one little job you two can do in the morning. I should get a shore squad in, as we are now in a UK port and therefore Union-minded, but there is not time; the Marine Superintendent is coming at eleven o'clock, so you'll have to be a bit circumspect. Have breakfast at eight, change and see me at half-past. Goodnight.'

Through standing up for the Chief Officer, I realised that two pint bottles of beer had gone to my head. There was only one thing to do: sit down and drink the third.

At ten o'clock my mate and I decided it was crash time; as we wandered back along the deck to our cabin, we decided that three pints of beer after a five-week dry period was enough, but very handy for an evening that had looked like being anti-climactic. Everything was quiet except for the periodic rattle of a train passing on the overhead railway.

Next morning, called by the night-watchman, we went through the usual routines including tea and toast in the pantry. It was strange to see the relief catering crew that had started at seven. New faces in the galley and new faces in the pantry who were not tight with the sugar, or even remarking on us taking neat shaky milk with our tea.

We ate a huge breakfast, asking for 'returns' on everything, and realised that the reason the beer had hit us so hard was that in the throes of docking we had forgotten to have the evening meal of the night before.

Working gear on, and report to the Chief Officer. The first thing my mate asked him was what circumspect meant.

'Well, sort of clandestine.'

'What's clandestine?'

'Well, softly, softly catchee monkey.'

We understood.

'Now,' said the Chief Officer, with a serious face, 'the hospital shithouse is blocked; I know what's happened. Somebody for some reason has been creeping in there for a crap and has not been giving a long enough flush to clean the pipe. The pipe runs a fair way on the deckhead of the starboard disused coal bunker. It's only a slight gradient, that's the trouble; there's a plug on the turn overboard, so it should be a simple job. O.K.?'

'Aye, aye, Sir,' we said; the answer 'aye, aye' is a handy reply. It does not mean yes or no, just that you have heard the order.

As we walked away, my mate said, 'A simple job? Is that better than his "nice little jobs"?'

I quoted one of Jan's favourite mangled sayings, 'The proof of the pudding will be in the size of the fuck-up!'

We started to collect scupper canes (circumspectly), spanners (clandestinely), mops and buckets (ostentatiously), down in the bunker space. While we were about the deck collecting, we noticed that stevedores were aboard, rigging the elevator pipes to discharge the bulk grain and derricks go take the bags. They all seemed to be called 'Wack' or 'La'. I wondered if there was some past French connection with Liverpool; my French master had always been on about two people called 'Des' and 'Les', who turned up in the most unlikely places; come to think about it, he had mentioned a person called 'La' many times.

Well! We started work on the pipe, standing on two boxes and after the usual struggle got the plug in the bend off and began probing and pulling with the screw on the end of the scupper cane, soon we started getting odd little bits out. A torch revealed nothing, but the stench was horrific; somebody had been eating birdsnest soup and ancient Chinese eggs. After about twenty minutes we thought we seemed to be pulling the main blockage towards us down the pipe.

We stopped and had a smoke.

About ten minutes later we climbed back onto our stools and started to pull the obstruction down toward us . . . Suddenly the cane came loose, and before we could jump clear the whole mass of shit, paper, bird's nest twigs and egg shells hit us.

But ugh!

On inspection of the situation, we found firstly that half of the mess had hit each of us, secondly that two cadets each half covered in shit smelled far worse than one cadet completely covered in shit, and thirdly the pipe was totally clear.

Next move was to clean the bunker space up, which thankfully took a shorter time than we expected. While we were doing this we discussed what to do with our impregnated clothing; jersey, trousers, shirt, underwear and socks were a different proposition from the gym shorts and shoes of the tropics. We decided that to walk straight under showers would be the most effective way;

afterwards to wrap the wet garments tightly in oilskins turned inside out, and take them home.

Having finished cleaning below, we got the buckets and tools, etc. on deck. The contents of the buckets was a difficult thing in broad daylight, but we espied on the quay a jubilee placed there for ships' rubbish, so we dumped the contents there; spread out it smelled 'orrible. So, both of us thinking the same thought we made a dive for the galley; there was a whole pile of ashes waiting to be dumped and we offered to do so for the Cook, and he happily agreed. As we left the galley, we heard him telling the Second Cook what nice, polite boys we were; poor sod!

We spread the ashes over the offending mess which immediately stopped smelling; the next job was to do the same for ourselves. But . . .

There was a shout from the deck. 'Come on up to the saloon,' yelled the Third Mate. 'The Shipping Master is waiting to close the Articles and you are the only ones left.' We reached the deck, and as we walked forr'd we checked that we were not dripping anything. Then we entered the heat of the accommodation and realised it made our smell even worse.

The Saloon had all the officialdom there; the Master, two from the Pool, the National Union of Seamen rep., two customs officers taking duty, a clerk from the agents, and a couple of nondescripts.

We walked across to the table where the Shipping Master sat; I just said, 'Cadets.' As he looked up he pulled a coloured handkerchief from his breast pocket and hovered it near his nose. I hoped for his sake it was scented – he looked a nice chap. The other occupants of the saloon vamoosed, with the exception of the Old Man. He stood transfixed; a look of deepening horror spreading over his face, at us and the stench that was growing in his beautiful saloon.

The Shipping Master looked at our discharge books and then

at our faces and said, 'Yes, you seem to be the same two that started the trip. OK.'

We made for the door before the speechless Old Man could muster any words. As we left, we heard the Shipping Master say cheerfully to the Old Man, 'Isn't it pleasant to smell two young men keeping the job going?'

Keeping The Job Going; we felt very proud of the compliment, even though it was probably made by a wise man in an attempt to stop the Old Man strangling us there and then!

I met Jan on deck, and he thrust an envelope into my hand. He had obviously been drinking this morning.

'Started already, Jan?' I laughed.

'Huh!' he muttered, 'I spent the night in the lee of bum island, and when I ask her for breakfast all she have is half a bottle of rum! I was just looking for you two.' He thrust an envelope into my hand. 'There you are, all the maritime terms you want for your exams. Quote it to the Captain who takes you for Orals; he don't ask you no more questions!'

Very often the more he drank, the better his English became; or it may have been the early morning rum. There was next to no hint of his usual gargle-gob stuff.

There was a clattering sound from behind us as the old bugger fell down the gangway; loaded ship, not far!

While we were cleaning up and changing into dry working gear, one of the taxi men appeared (he heard the word taxi and was quick to point out that they weren't taxis but private hire cars; this, apparently under some Liverpool by-law made it legal) asking where we were going.

My mate said London, I said East Anglia. He said quickly, 'London's easy. East Anglia, you want the Harwich Boat Train, goes down through Norfolk and Suffolk.'

We asked him how much, and he just laughed and said, 'We

never hurt anybody, we want your business next trip as well.' He was quite right and I used him for transport in Liverpool for years afterwards, and sometimes he did some quite complicated drivings for me.

Changed, we decided to see the Chief Officer; it was quiet in the ship, apart from cargo work and people starting to take the Christmas Tree down before it fell down.

We tapped on his door.

'Come in,' was shouted.

We entered and noted that he was seated at his desk, with his jacket undone, a glass of beer in hand, and mail from home on his desk. We fervently hoped that it contained happy and cheerful news for the old bastard!

'We were wondering about leave, Sir,' we said.

'Leave?' he shouted. 'Leave? You've only been away from home five and a half months!'

As the Third Officer had prophesied, it was a masterful performance. He went on to list our sins of omission, commission, transmission, and every other sort of bloody mission, except the Seamen's Mission, but of course the Old Man had covered that in B.A.

He told us we could go on leave, but to be back certainly by the time stated on the telegram. 'If you are not back by then, which will be the signing-on time, you will probably be messing the Master and the Shipping Master about. What will happen is that on the next leave you have you'll be called back twenty-four hours earlier, because you've shown yourselves to be unreliable.'

He made a gesture of dismissal and turned back to his desk. It was then that my bloody mate risked blowing the whole bloody works.

'Please, Sir, we've washed out those gloves you lent us; but they are drying; we'll let you have them first thing next trip.'

The Chief Officer did not turn round, but spat venomously over his shoulder,
'Piss off!'

APPENDIX I

The contents of the envelope which Jan handed me on pay-off day.

The *Bolivar*

A twin screw brig, with an A1 rig
Was the good ship *Bolivar*.
She was spick and span from the Donkeyman
To the bilge on the capstan bar.

We were pulley hauled, with a ten foot yaul,
And a regular shanty crew,
Right avast, at the sheerstrake mast,
The scarlet bosun flew.

We hugged the shore, for a month or more,
Till on the second night,
From out of the gloom the twartships boom
Of the *Deutschland* hove in sight.

Then, inch by inch, as she dipped her winch
With her fidlies flying high
Through the fog and mist with a forrard list
She strove to pass us by.

'Full speed ahead', our Captain said;
We heard the pennants crack,
As with a flick of his heel he put the wheel
Abeam on the starboard tack.

Then, bilge in hand, he took his stand
Upon the tafrail hatch,
And the *Bolivar*, like a shooting star,
Began to roar and ratch.

For an hour or two in the weathering glue
We steamed in line astray,
Then the sails ran dry in our engine fly
And the draught marks blew away.

And inch by inch as she dipped her winch
With her fidlies flying high
Through the fog and mist, with a forrard list
The *Deutschland* passed us by.